Love Is
Your Disguise

---

*Second Lesson Sermons
For Lent/Easter
Cycle A*

Frank Luchsinger

Dear Irma,
Thank you for your help with this
and for sharing with us your
wonderful loving spirit. ☺
Blessings to you always.
Frank

CSS Publishing Company, Inc., Lima, Ohio

LOVE IS YOUR DISGUISE

Copyright © 1997 by
CSS Publishing Company, Inc.
Lima, Ohio

Scripture quotations are from the *Revised Standard Version of the Bible*, copyrighted 1946, 1952 © 1971, 1973, by the Division of Christian Education of the National Council of the Churches of Christ in the USA. Used by permission.

Library of Congress Cataloging-in-Publication Data

Luchsinger, Frank, 1954-
    Love is your disguise : second lesson sermons for Lent/Easter, cycle A / Frank Luchsinger.
        p.   cm.
    Includes bibliographical references.
    ISBN 0-7880-1269-X (pbk. : alk. paper)
    1. Lenten sermons. 2. Holy-Week sermons. 3 Easter—Sermons. 4. Bible. N.T. Epistles—Sermons. 5. United Methodist Church (U.S.)—Sermons. 6. Sermons, American. I. Title.
BV4277.L77   1998
252'.62—dc21   98-13655
                                                                        CIP

This book is available in the following formats, listed by ISBN:
    0-7880-1269-X   Book
    0-7880-1270-3   IBM
    0-7880-1271-1   MAC
    0-7880-1271-X   Sermon Prep

PRINTED IN U.S.A.

To Beth

love is your disguise

Acknowledgments

In preparing these sermons, I am indebted to many. To Georgia Shirey, who worked tirelessly to prepare the manuscript and who served as an invaluable sounding board, and to Elizabeth Shirey for valuable editorial assistance; to Bud Leskovac, my partner in ministry, who shoulders marvelously the responsibilities of the Master's Church; to the staff team with whom I am privileged to be in ministry; to the congregation of Church of the Master at Otterbein College, which consistently inspires and kindly receives my preaching; to my family, beloved Beth to whom this book is dedicated and our boys, Joe and Adam; and to God, who was, and is, and is to come; my deep and abiding thanks.

Without you, friends, I would have neither the creativity nor the energy for projects such as this.

May Christ Easter in you as you reach for higher and deeper things.

Love Is Your Disguise invites the reader into the biblical texts and the Gospel proclamation with the creative correlating of the sacred story with the stories of human beings. The careful and vast use of historical and modern events from life situations both excite and draw the reader into that place of the heart and mind where the Gospel can be heard anew. Dr. Luchsinger has given us a gift of scholarship, pastoral sensitivity, and artistic merit.

> C. Joseph Sprague
> Bishop, United Methodist Church
> Chicago Area, Northern Illinois Conference
> Chicago, Illinois

Bright, perceptive, eloquent, committed ... Frank Luchsinger is all of these and much, much more. In this book (which by the way would be an excellent study book for the seasons of Lent and Eastertide), Frank calls us to look at life with resurrection eyes.

> James W. Moore
> Senior Pastor
> St. Luke's United Methodist Church
> Houston, Texas

Frank Luchsinger is a preacher's preacher. He is able to give expression to the truths of the Gospel in ways that engage the listener's mind, heart, and spirit. This book of sermons gives clear illustrations about how God's love that comes into the world can be received in such way that people will receive and act. In addition to being one of our graduates, Frank teaches homiletics as adjunct faculty. Any preacher thinking about the start of the Church Year will find this book of sermons to be quite helpful.

> Norman E. Dewire
> President
> Methodist Theological School in Ohio
> Delaware, Ohio

Table Of Contents

Introduction

Writing these sermons was for me a blessing, an adventure, and a terrific combination of challenge and enjoyment. Preparing to preach on the second lesson for Lent and Easter called me forth to unexpected pathways and destinations. The consideration of our inheritance as Christians, and the questions of *peace in the midst of suffering* and *new birth in Christ* are central to the traditional faith. Less anticipated were *God's Blessed Forgetting* and our *Holy Emptiness*; surely this has been a time of growth for this preacher, and likewise I pray that these offerings will be helpful to you in your walk.

These biblical letters of love and encouragement were written to people trying to start a church, some of whom were experiencing great torment by Roman persecutors. In those days the church had problems and the individual followers of Jesus had problems (sound familiar?). So it is a wonderful challenge and freedom for the preacher through these letters to address issues of vital importance to the church, the individual, the family, and the community.

Beginning with Easter I have begun a consideration of Christian living, which I suppose is a never ending one. How will the Church be and how will Christians be in a time which always claims Easter as its season: We know the end of the story and yet we are in the midst of the story; we know we are claimed by Christ and yet it would seem most of the time Christ has some additional claiming to do. Easter is a time for higher and deeper things. We experience with thankfulness the undefeated power of God and long to know more of God's unexplainable, but manifest vigor. And yet we know that this is also the God of the "still small voice" and that we meet this God in surprising places, not only in high holy places, but also in out of the way places with the most unlikely of people. In this series we will meet a handful of these people, maybe even some people we all know.

So bless you in your reading and in your journeying and may Christ Easter in us always.

Love Is
Your Disguise

2 Corinthians 5:20b—6:10

The pastor of a village church has been given a high honor to judge the costume contest. First there will be a parade through town; the high school band leading in a "doo-dah" band fashion, which means no straight lines or formations: band members at times leaving the procession altogether to greet friends and family along the way. And then hundreds of children following in costume. This precarious honor is high risk, for the pastor knows that some of these children, barely recognizable to him, attend his church and are hoping to win one of the prizes to be given later at the fairgrounds. "I watched them all go by; several looked like costume-prize contenders," he observed.

At the fairgrounds the judges are almost settled on the first prize: a little girl dressed up as a burlap sack of potatoes, the spuds made from stuffed nylons, soft and puckered like fifteen small cabbage patch kids peaking out of the sack.

Noticing that the judges' attention is settling on Patty Potato, another contender calls out, "Wait, look over here!" It is the boy in the fried egg costume. It is a cute costume, but a fried egg walking down the street, though an unusual sight, makes one think of break-fast at the local diner rather than a prize-winning children's costume. "Watch this," he says. Lying flat on the asphalt, he spreads his arms and legs like a child ready to make a snow angel and by vibrating his limbs, makes the egg "sizzle" in subtle ripples. There in the park on that fall afternoon, the egg actually fries right on the blacktop. "I can almost smell the bacon," a judge laughs. The kid in the fried egg suit wins the prize because when he finally got the judges' attention, he made a good impression.

Make A Good Impression

Some have made a life of making good impressions.

In the 1950s Ferdinand Demara lived an interesting life as a surgeon, a dentist, a professor, a psychologist, a deputy sheriff, and a prison warden. As a young man, after spending a couple of years in a monastery, Ferdinand Demara enlisted in the United States Army. One of his friends in the service invited him to come home on leave, where Ferdinand was shown the soldier's impressive collection of certificates and diplomas, which he had earned through many years of schooling. On another visit to the same soldier's home, Demara took the credentials and later assumed the identity of his friend.

After subsequently enlisting in the United States Navy, he received first aid training. Later, Demara obtained the credentials of a psychologist, Dr. R. L. French, and began a teaching position at a school operated by a Catholic order. After a time, Demara was discovered and fired. This lead to Demara's training for the priesthood in Chicago and then, with the help of Dr. French's identity, he secured a position as Dean of the School of Philosophy at Ganon College, Erie, Pennsylvania. But here too Demara was exposed. After his time in Pennsylvania, he found his way to Washington, D.C., where he managed a center for students in need of psychological counseling. He later secured the appointment as deputy sheriff, but the background investigation revealed his criminal past. After serving eighteen months in prison for having deserted the Navy during wartime, Ferdinand enrolled in a Boston law school, leaving after a year for Maine where he took a position as a biology professor. While at the college he stole the academic credentials of Dr. Joseph Cyr, which lead Ferdinand to enlist as a surgeon lieutenant in the Royal Canadian Navy. During this time he performed difficult operations including the removal of a bullet lodged near the heart of a wounded sailor. Word of Dr. Cyr's medical talents spread and Demara's masquerade was discovered. Again on the road, Demara's travels lead him to Huntsville, Texas, where, as Ben Jones, he served as prison warden. Demara sold his story to *Life* magazine, "but the publicity became too much for him when a prisoner recognized Demara's profile on the magazine, then a book, then a movie, and for Demara so much exposure meant that he was forced to use his real name for the remainder of his life."[1] Demara became a master of disguise by hiding behind the identities and credentials of others.

Some are considered masters of disguise because they know how to disguise the appearance of others. Tony Mendez was such a person. An "exfiltration" expert during the height of the Cold War, Tony's job often involved helping a Soviet spy/defector escape to the West: such was the case in February 1970. Mendez was given the job of getting a Soviet spy/defector out of the Asian country where he was based. The defector's appearance was well known and the KGB was on his trail; a clever disguise was needed. The solution to the disguise problem turned out to be surprisingly simple: a big cigar.

"This guy had no false beard, no false glasses, no false mustache, a slight change of hair style," Mendez said. "But he was given a cigar, a very good cigar, and he was taught how to smoke it."[2] At the airport the defector blew smoke in the eyes of the security officer reviewing his documents. Abruptly the documents were returned, sending the spy safely on his way.

Some are masters of disguise because they know how to change the appearance of others. Some are masters of disguise because they are impersonators or impressionists. And I have noticed that when impressionists meet the subject of their impression, there is often an awkward silence: when facsimile meets fact, the one who claims to be and the one who is.

Love Is Your Disguise

So at the beginning of Lent, as we start our journey of introspection and preparation for the holiest season of the church year, we ask ourselves the question: Are we facsimile or fact? We know that, though saved, we are afflicted; though claimed, we have hardships; though restored, we have calamities and tumults and labor and hunger. So in this time of introspection and preparation, we want to know: Are we facsimile or fact? And we know the answer — we are both. It is *because* we follow Christ, *because* we have

11

been claimed by him, that we put on a disguise and wear it, the life-altering garment of love.

Recorded a few years ago by Radar Rose, a little known Appalachian Folkrock group, the song "Love Is Your Disguise" begins:

> *I know what you want from me,*
> *I can see it in your eyes,*
> *You've come when I need you most,*
> *and love is your disguise ...*[3]

It is as if the lyricists are writing of their first encounter with Christ. He comes to us wearing the garment of love and invites us to wear this life-altering garment as well. For him it is not a disguise but simply more evidence of his nature; for us simply wearing the garment of love makes us better and more beautiful. Jesus wears love perfectly, as a seamless garment, but *this garment shapes us* and even changes who we understand ourselves to be as we wear it. And as his garment is shaping us, making us, we are at once both facsimile and fact until we, the object of his shaping and making, are made perfect in his love.

Paul advises working together with Christ. Do not accept the grace of God in vain. "Put no obstacle in anyone's way...." It is the rule for the Christian as it is the rule in medicine: "First, do no harm." Though we are tired and afflicted, though we have beatings and tumults, labor and hunger, we have not by these things earned the right to harm. We have not earned, in our weariness, the right to degrade and disparage those near to us. We have not earned the right, through hardship, to forsake kindness and genuine love. We have not, through tumults, labor and hunger, earned the right to forsake purity, knowledge, truthfulness, and the power of God. Though we may be treated as impostors, let us always be true. Though treated as unknown, as nothing, yet we are well known and possess everything. And though treated as poor, we are making many rich.

So as we embark upon this season of introspection, let us consider the God-giveness of our names and of our lives. How many names have we been given and by whom? Have we enjoyed the credentials earned by another? Have we found a garment to wear which makes us, shapes us, saves us? Have we been impressed by nails and thorns and the cross upon his back? The One who comes carves away with kinder hands, more loving than the hands of the best surgeon; injured hands but also precise, those things close to our heart which are unwanted, damaging, unhelpful — those things which threaten life. And when he is through, all that remains is healing and hope, focus and freedom, power and purpose, and evidence of the One who has been attending us in our need, shaping us, making us, saving us. It is his will that we make a good impression with our lives, a good impression with our living, that we make a strong impression even on these pathways, even in these days, so that some will say because of the impression, the good impression of our feet upon the path, there is evidence here that he has come this way — the One who came to save.

---

1. *Gazette*: A Royal Canadian Mounted Police publication by Corporal Michael Duncan RCMP, Economic Crime Branch, Headquarters, Ottawa, 1996.

2. *Detroit Free Press,* Sept. 18, 1997.

3. Jane Gabrielle and Sony Campbell, lyrics and music, "Love Is Your Disguise," album *Dog Years,* Five Flat Records 111, 1992.

A Bigger Peace

Romans 5:12-19

There is only one cupcake left and there are two little girls. "I want the bigger piece! ..." and as soon as she says it she knows her mother's next words. Placing a knife on the table her mom says, "One cuts, the other one gets to choose." So the elaborate process begins — one daughter trying to cut the cupcake exactly in half to prevent her sister from having "the bigger piece." How honest children are!

Adults are more subtle when they desire the bigger piece. Though often not stated and not always concerned with a commodity which can be held in the hand, much of what drives modern life is a desire *for a bigger piece.* The urge to dominate and possess may well date to a time when primitive humans dwelt in caves and, after the hunt, fought over a bigger slab of meat. In our times Standard Oil became successful and large enough under the guidance of John D. Rockefeller that anti-trust laws were instituted. Leaders were afraid of the piece Standard Oil already had and worried that a bigger piece would damage competition and discourage commerce. Consider the displacement of Native Americans. Whenever agreement or tranquillity on the topic of "land" seemed to be established, settlers became motivated by a desire for a bigger piece, a different piece, the Native American piece.

Consider the Oklahoma land rush of 1889. Authorized by President Benjamin Harrison, unoccupied lands of the Indian territory were opened to white settlement. On April 22, 1889, at noon a gunshot served as a signal to settlers to cross over the border to stake their claims. Almost two million acres of tribal land were transformed into thousands of individual land claims within nine hours. However, many of the more desirable plots were taken by "Sooners" — those who had crossed into the territory sooner than permitted seeking a better piece.

Or think of the tensions in the Middle East. It's easy to understand the desire of nations to provide a homeland for the persecuted Jews. Where better to locate such a gathering of the brutalized and dispossessed than in their historical home — Palestine. One problem: people already lived there. Thus, the plan has been riddled with conflict, and the hills and roads once walked by the Prince of Peace have not been very peaceful.

Or consider the tragic phenomenon known as "festival seating" at rock concerts where no one in fact really has an assigned seat, but those who can push and claw and trample their way to the front are given preferred locations from which to view the concert. Why do professional athletes in our times always have agents? Because they want a bigger piece. It used to be that most of the big money in professional sports went to team owners and television company shareholders but not to the players. It seemed reasonable to many that things were out of balance. But now the balance is 100 million dollar contracts for professional basketball players, and more than a few wonder why. When does the reasonable desire for a bigger piece become unreasonable, and when does our desire to hoard, to possess, and to dominate become an affront to the Giver of all good gifts?

Is it safe to say that the desire for a bigger piece causes some among us to become "Sooners" to take unfair advantage simply to own a bigger piece or to possess bigger influence?

One thing is sure: to possess a bigger piece does not ensure that we will be possessed by a bigger *peace*. In the fourteenth chapter of John, Jesus says, "Peace I leave with you; my peace I give to you; not as the world gives do I give to you. Let not your hearts be troubled, neither let them be afraid." So Jesus gives peace, leaves peace, not as the world gives but as God gives peace. But in a world which strives for a bigger piece, often with vigor, a bigger peace is found in fleeting moments.

16

In our text from Romans, we find Paul, the teacher, explaining how from Adam's act of disobedience has come the curse of sin, and by Christ's act of obedience has come the gift of life. He summarizes, "Then as one man's trespass led to condemnation for all men, so one man's act of righteousness leads to acquittal and life for all men. For as by one man's disobedience many were made sinners, so by one man's obedience many will be made righteous" (Romans 5:18-19).

We who are both disobedient and obedient, who hear the voices which call us to pursue a bigger piece and sometimes follow those voices but also hear Christ's voice, the voice of the Prince of Peace, we know the anxious feelings of the disciples who were riding with Jesus in the boat on the Sea of Galilee, where storms so easily stir up. They saw him exhausted, sleeping in the back of the boat while the storm was lashing about them, the waves crashing over the sides of the boat so violently that they thought for sure they would all perish. We with them come running to Jesus without any remembrance of the peace which passes understanding saying, "Lord, do you not care if we perish?" We live in that moment where we have enough trust to call upon him, to call upon his name, and yet we also live in a moment where we know if he does not awaken quickly from sleep to calm the storm we all may be washed overboard. We feel his rebuke at our faithlessness as we have called upon him once again, forgetting his prior assurances, and hear him command the waters as only one rudely awakened from sleep can, saying, "Peace, be still," and the waves fall silent.

We remember the disciples again in a boat. Jesus comes to them walking on the water and at first they think he is a ghost, but he assures them he is not. Then Peter calls out to answer Jesus, "Lord, if it is you, bid me to come to you on the water," as if it is Peter's prerogative to stand where Jesus stands and walk where Jesus walks. But Jesus says to him, "Come." So, getting out of the boat, Peter walks out upon the water and comes to Jesus. But Peter sees the wind and becomes afraid. Beginning to sink he cries out, "Lord, save me!" Immediately Jesus' hand reaches out and catches Peter as he says to him, "O, man of little faith, why did you doubt?" They get into the boat and peace comes upon wind and wave.

Oh how perilous it is for us when we claim for ourselves the prerogative of God, as if we need a bigger piece, as if we need to claim for ourselves the owner's manual for our town, for our land, for our home, for our world. Oh, how perilous it is for us to claim for ourselves what is truly the prerogative of God. We seek to tame the wind and we cannot tame it. We seek to move the mountain and we cannot move it. We seek to heal the sick and by our power cannot heal them. We seek to ensure a land flowing in milk and honey, truly to build the land of promise, but we cannot build it because of our broken promises. We seek to find peace, but we cannot find it because we pursue a bigger piece. And if we find peace, we can only catch a glimpse of it.

We are like Mary in the garden of Christ's resurrection. She has come to anoint the body of our crucified Lord but has discovered an empty tomb. She runs back to Simon Peter and the other disciple, saying to them through her tears, "They have taken our Lord out of the tomb and we do not know where they have laid him." We, too, come seeking the crucified Christ, sometimes with tears seeking a bigger peace, and we do not know where to find it.

We are like the disciples gathered after his crucifixion with the door shut because of their fear. Jesus comes and stands among them and says, "Peace be with you." And we are slow to accept that one so ravaged by earthly powers and principalities has in fact overcome the world, and we are like Thomas, doubting until Christ places our hand in his wounded flesh. Then he says to us, "Peace be with you and as the Father has sent me, even so I send you." We realize that *his* peace is a bigger peace. Bigger than the peace which calms the heart and soothes the spirit. It is bigger than the fleeting peace which offers hope in time of trouble or healing assurance, or peace which comes when we determine to redirect our life energy from the endless pursuit of a bigger piece, something which can be held in the hand. It is more than simply a calming sense of well-being or an inner repose. The bigger peace of Christ is the blessed assurance that comes when we trust God, understand our access to Him, and believe that our lives can be used meaningfully in serving God's purposes. We do not seek peace as if it were a safe harbor, a paradise of tranquillity and calm, an idol to which all else must be sacrificed. For when Jesus said he came not to bring peace but a sword this is what he means. He comes to assail such notions that our ultimate goal is tranquillity. He shows us that we live in a world of storm *and* calm, and that God's peace is present in both. In this lesson we find confidence in knowing that God is the God of wind and wave, *and* the God of calm, the God of tumult, *and* the God of tranquillity. The bigger peace of Christ is the peace which turns over to God God's rightful place and receives thankfully our rightful place in His presence. Sing to the glory of God, O you saints, for there is a bigger peace which rests upon you in times of joy and in times of anguish, in times of faith and in times of doubt, in times of hope and in times of despair. Paul writes in Romans 15, "May the God of hope fill you with all joy and peace in believing, so that by the power of the Holy Spirit, you may abound in hope." Abound in hope when you are able and trust in the promise which you have received. "Behold, the dwelling place of God is with men. He will dwell with them, and they shall be His people, and God Himself will be with them; He will wipe away every tear from their eyes and death shall be no more, neither shall there be mourning nor crying nor pain anymore ..." And the Lord said, "Behold, I make all things new" (Revelation 21:3-5). So seek and receive, people of God, your bigger peace. Come into God's presence with singing. God, the Ultimate One, has dominion both in time of storm *and* in time of tranquillity. Receive from Him your holy welcome which is, in all things, peace.

Inherit The World

Romans 4:1-5, 13-17

"The promise to Abraham and his descendants, that they should inherit the world, did not come through the law but through the righteousness of faith," so writes Paul in Romans. Abraham was a man of righteous faith but, as you know, Abraham wasn't always *Abraham, the father of many nations;* he was Abram who became Abraham. He got a new name, and this isn't unique only to him.

Samuel Clemmons, apprentice steamboat pilot and printer, became "Mark Twain," which is a riverman's term for water two fathoms deep, or to say it another way, water barely safe for navigation.

In 1882, a baby girl caught a high fever and nearly died. She survived but lost both sight and sound. Blinded at nineteen months, she grew to become Helen Keller, the world famous author and speaker.

A young Ehrich Weiss found release from Budapest. As an adult he found release from everything else — Harry Houdini.

John Newton sailed slave ships, delivering human commodity to the new world. Later he wrote the lyrics for the hymn "Amazing Grace."

The foster son of a Thembu chief, raised in the tribal culture of South Africa and imprisoned for more than 25 years, became the nation's Nobel Prize winning president, Nelson Mandella.

Mohandas was the husband in an arranged marriage when he was age thirteen. Sent to London to study law, he later became interested in the rights of the Indian people. He became Gandhi.

Saul, the persecutor of Christians, became Paul, the evangelist to the world.

Simon, son of John, fisher of fish, became Cephas or Peter, fisher of men, follower of Jesus, the Rock upon which Christ built his Church.

And Abram, called at age 75 to strike out for the land of promise, became Abraham, father of many nations, because he was *faithful* to God.

So as Paul writes, "Abraham believed God, and it was reckoned to him as righteousness." Abraham believed in what God had revealed and received the world as an inheritance. But was the world any more an inheritance to Abraham than it is to us? And if it is for us as it was for Abraham to inherit the world, how can this, and how will this, be done? Paul again writes, "The promise to Abraham and his descendants, that they should inherit the world, did not come through the law but through the righteousness of faith." And if this is true, is it not also true that the law to which we are subject, the law which restrains, is the law of our low expectations of what God can do in our world; the law of the low expectations of what the power of God can use in our midst; the law of the low expectations of what God can do in us and through us for the reclamation of all of God's children and for the reclamation of the world for this time and for all time?

After Jesus has been arrested, he stands before Pilate, the world's judgment standing poised to bring its wrath upon him. Pilate asks Jesus in chapter 18 of John, "So you are a king?" and Jesus answers, "You say that I am a king. For this I was born, and for this I have come into the world, to bear witness to the truth. Every one who is of the truth hears my voice." Pilate asks him, "What is truth?" And Pilate's question echoes throughout the ages. It is a question for us today. What is truth? What is the law of truth to which we give our allegiance? Which Truth of the many truths will be the ultimate Truth for us? For Abram it was the Truth of God as revealed to him, the Truth which called him. It was very far into his life journey to set out for the land of promise and to become the father of many nations because he heard God's voice and was faithful to what he heard. But that is what Abram did, without regard to age, without regard to hardship, without regard to comfort, without regard to conventional wisdom.

In the year 1925 at Dayton, Tennessee, there was a battle over "truth" being waged in a courthouse during two sweltering weeks of July. Famous attorneys were doing battle over "what is truth?" A 24-year-old science teacher/football coach had been teaching evolution, and the fundamentalist South was exercised. How did the world come into being? How was it created? What role did God play? Is the Bible true? were questions flying about. A southern law against teaching evolution was being challenged in the courts, and a circus/county fair atmosphere enveloped this small Tennessee mining town as the world's attention focused on the town and the question, "What is truth?" Modestly fictionalized in a 1960 film, conservative prosecuting attorney Matthew Harrison Brady, after being asked by defense attorney Henry Drummond, "How old do you think this rock is?" proclaims "I am more interested in the Rock of Ages than I am in the age of rocks!" And for us gathered here today and for the people of God in general, we are equally concerned with "What is truth?"

If we are to inherit the world then how will we inherit it, and what will be the nature of our inheritance? How will we hear God's voice and understand God's revelation? How will we set out for lands promising and inviting, and how will we be in partnership with God in our living and in our stewardship of the God-giveness of all that is, so that others will find the world to come promising, inviting, and hospitable?

Abram set out because he had heard God's voice and understood what he heard to be Truth. He set out for a place which God revealed to be good, and because he followed and because he listened, he became Abraham, the father of many nations; he became the fruitful one. He was blessed and was a blessing to many nations who looked to him as "patriarch, father, source" but not The Source.

So how shall we go forth and what will be our Truth? Is the Bible true? Even today there is much discussion about how the universe was created. Through our scripture, much is revealed about God's will and about persons who struggled and lived

23

faithfully, who became great examples and teachers of how God would have us live. In our Bible we receive great teaching, lessons, and insights, and we also learn much about how the people of faith 3000 years ago understood their world.

But for us, in this time, the question is not whether or not we will be more interested in the Rock of Ages than in the age of rocks; it is a question of whether we will be faithful to the Rock of Ages *and* interested in the age of rocks. Where will we find our Truth? We will find our Truth in the scriptures and in all of the multifaceted ways that God reveals Truth to us, about our world, about ourselves, and about God's desire for us in our living. We do not reject temporal knowledge in favor of eternal knowledge. Rather temporal knowledge is a part of eternal knowledge as fragmented, as incomplete, as imperfect as is the state of our current understanding. It continues to be a part of what God is revealing to us. We use temporal knowledge within the frame of eternal Truth.

Our native American friends have a saying: *We do not inherit the world from our grandparents, but rather we borrow the world from our grandchildren.*[1] God's promise to Abram who became Abraham was that he and his descendants would inherit the world. And likewise to us and to our descendants, it is God's promise that we will inherit the world. We have inherited the world, and we will pass the world to our descendants as an inheritance. Which is to say, it is not given to us to be used up as a disposable commodity but rather given to us as a trust, and therefore we are given a name: steward, trustee, guardian, caregiver. And so we must ask, how will the world and all that abides therein be passed along to those who come after? How can we pass along what is best, what is right, what is wise, what is beautiful, what is true? Listen to the voices of those who have gone before us, and be guided by their learning as much as by our own. Listen to the ones who will come after us and be guided by their needs as much as by our own. Listen to the voice of God, to the voice of eternal Truth, as revealed in the scriptures and elsewhere, and let God's desire, God's hope, God's love always be the divine frame by which the picture of our living is shaped.

24

Jesus tells the story:

The kingdom of heaven will be like when a man going on a journey calls together his servants and entrusts to them his property. To one he gives five talents, to another two and to another one, to each according to his ability.

Immediately the one with five talents trades them and makes five talents more; likewise the servant with two talents makes two talents more, but the servant who has received one talent digs a hole in the ground and hides his master's money.

After a long time the master of those servants returns to settle accounts with them.

He who received the five talents comes forward, bringing five talents more, saying, "Master, you delivered to me five talents; here I have made five talents more."

And the master says to him, "Well done, good and faithful servant; you have been faithful over a little, I will set you over much; enter into the joy of your master."

Also the one who had two talents comes forward, saying, "Master, you delivered to me two talents; here I have made two talents more."

The master says to him, "Well done, good and faithful servant; you have been faithful over a little, I will set you over much; enter into the joy of your master."

Now he who had received the one talent comes forward, saying, "Master, I know you to be a hard man, reaping where you did not sow, and gathering where you did not winnow; so I was afraid, and I went and hid your talent in the ground. Here you have what is yours."

But his master answered him, "You wicked and slothful servant! You knew that I reap where I have not sowed, and gather where I have not winnowed? Then you ought to have invested my money with the bankers, and at my coming I should have received what was my own with interest. So take the talent from him, and give it to him who has the ten talents. For to every one who has will more be given, and he will have abundance; but from him who has not, even what he has will be taken away ..."
(Matthew 25:14-30, author paraphrase)

And so it will be that one day God will desire to know what is the condition of that which has been inherited, when we will come to the Master to return what has been borrowed. There is a great temptation to think: what we have is ours to dispose of as we will. But in our hearts we know better, and one day the Master, the owner, will return to take stock of our stewardship. Let us listen to the voices of those who have gone before us and be guided by their learning as much as by our own. Let us listen to the ones who will come after us and be guided by their needs as much as by our own. Let us listen to the voice of God, to the voice of eternal Truth, as revealed in the scriptures and elsewhere, and let us let God's desire, God's hope, God's love always be the divine frame by which the picture of our living is shaped. If we can do these things seeking to partner with God in fulfilling God's will and purposes in the living of these days, then we too will be given a new name. We, with Abraham, will be called "Faithful." *Inherit the world* and in so doing, be *faithful*.

---

1. Herb Miller, Speech, Church of the Master, Westerville, Ohio, November 5, 1996

Enter Your Pax Word
A Lenten Lexicon

Text: Romans 5:1-11

$\mathbf{Enter}$ your password — flashed up on the computer screen. The pastor was trying to show some of his parishioners the church's new web page. With pride he had gathered them into his office after the Christian Education Committee meeting. He paused. "I don't do this very often ... We may have to try this another time," he said disappointed. "Try 'church,'" someone says, looking over his shoulder. The pastor types *c - h - u - r - c - h*. Amazingly the internet connection pops up on the screen. A password is a secret word given to gain entry. It can mean security. But if you can't remember the password, you can be out of luck. So folks choose easy passwords they think they can remember. The church uses "church." The financial secretary of the church uses his/her first name. On your home security system you use your birthday for your password number. This practice increases ease of entry and decreases security, in other words, defeats the purpose. But does it defeat the purpose any more than having a password so difficult, it can almost never be remembered?

Enter your pax word. In Lent we seek a different kind of entry which requires a different word — a pax word. The fifth chapter of Romans is famous for the powerful words Paul employs: grace, saved, reconciled, bled, suffering, weak, die, wrath. It is hard to appreciate the power of carefully chosen words in an age when we throw words around so easily and with little precision.

When I was a boy and my parents were teaching table manners, we would be instructed to fork reasonable amounts of food into our months rather than to use the fork as a shovel, passing the

27

maximum load limit. This was such a hard lesson to learn and it took parents years to teach it to three ravenous boys at very different ages and stages of development that the instruction gradually became shorter: "Please remember to use your fork properly," became, "That's too big a bite," which became "That'sabigbite." My father could insert, "That'sabigbite," into a sentence without diverting his thought or breaking his cadence of conversation. "We won't be able to go to Aunt Mary's That'sabigbite this weekend because we have to trim the trees."

But times have changed and now I am the parent and my boys are learning table manners. "Don't use your fork as a shovel," still comes up from time to time, but, "That'sabigbite," has become passe. "That'sa**mega**bite," I instruct without breaking the cadence of my conversation. And at times I am tempted to employ "Gigabite."

Or consider how a person from just a generation ago would interpret our strange use of words. "She shot a trey" — she shot a basketball from behind the three point arc.

Q: "What kind of jeans are those?"

A: "Guess."

Or the possible definitions for these terms: *white-out* — a weather condition; *ink-jet* — a dark plane; *microwave* — a special kind of hair permanent; *compact disk* — similar to a ruptured disc; and *P C* — a pea soup colored body of water.

Remember when Jesus was preparing to enter Jerusalem? To his disciples he said, "Go find me a colt. And if the owners say, 'Why are you untying the colt?' give them the word, 'The Lord has need of it.' " And the disciples did as Jesus instructed and there was a great parade — people throwing their garments on the road, lifting their voices, "Blessed is the King who comes in the name of the Lord!" But some of the Pharisees chastised Jesus because of the commotion and the disciples' excitement, "Teacher, rebuke your disciples!" And drawing near to Jerusalem Jesus responded, "If these were silent the very stones would cry out." If the followers of Jesus were silent, the very stones would be given words to shout. Then as you recall, Jesus saw the city and wept

28

over it. "Would that even today you knew the things that make for peace!" (Luke 19: 30-42).

What is your pax word? Paul writes, "Since we are justified by faith, we have peace with God through our Lord Jesus Christ. Through him we have obtained access to the grace in which we stand and we rejoice in our hope of sharing the glory of God." What is your pax word and how does it give you access to this grace in which we stand? In Lent we think of words employed here by Paul, suffering, blood, weak, die, but for most of us it is difficult to claim the suffering of Jesus which seems remote and over with. Even his disciples, present at the time, ran away from it, but each one later returned to make his or her own sacrifice of suffering in his name. The suffering in Vietnamese POW camps or of political prisoners in unknown dungeons was no greater than Christ's suffering during his last days, and yet it is repelling to us and thankfully we see his suffering at a distance. But to say that because it is remote from us, in time, then also that it is completed, over with, once and for all accomplished, is to diminish the power of his presence and the vigilance of his love.

> *Jesus said: "I was hungry and you gave me food, I was thirsty and you gave me drink, I was a stranger and you welcomed me, I was naked and you clothed me, I was sick and you visited me, I was in prison and you came to me." Then the righteous will answer him. "Lord, when did we see thee hungry and feed thee, or thirsty and give thee drink? And when did we see thee a stranger and welcome thee or naked and clothe thee? And when did we see thee sick or in prison and visit thee?" And the king will answer them, "Truly, I say to you, as you did it to one of the least of these my brethren, you did it to me."*
> — Matthew 25: 35-40

And so his suffering is not complete, it is not over with, it is not accomplished. As the world groans so our Savior continues to groan, crucified again and again on unknown Calvarys, laid to rest in graves unmarked. In this season we employ a lexicon unique to our faith: upper room, towel, mortification, hand washing, thorn, cup, loaf. The Word becomes flesh and dwells among us.

"Since we are justified by faith, we have peace with God through our Lord Jesus Christ. Through him we have obtained access to this grace in which we stand...." And because you have a pax word, you have obtained access. But how have you used this access? How have you claimed this access? Do you know your pax word? The apostle Paul in Romans 5 also uses other words: faith, hope, love, poured, reconciled.

A pastor is traveling in September of '97. On a Saturday morning, he hurriedly readies himself in a hotel room for a busy day. Putting on a well-starched shirt he flips on the television. "Oh, I forgot," he thinks out loud, "Princess Di is being buried today." And pausing he observes the dignitaries and the choirs and the honor guard. He watches as the Archbishop of Canterbury invites all who are present to pray and all who are listening and viewing the service to pray: "Our Father, who art in heaven, hallowed be thy name ..." The camera cuts to the multitude gathered outside the church, " ... Thy will be done, on earth as it is in heaven ..." The pastor alone in his hotel room prays out loud as well," Give us this day our daily bread, forgive us our trespasses even as we forgive those who trespass against us...." The prayer over, he blushes with a pang of embarrassment as he realizes the service with which he has been praying out loud is on tape delay. But then he thinks, "How many others around the globe in many time zones as the service is rebroadcast and rebroadcast will likewise pray this great prayer, sending it echoing throughout God's created world? And may it be so, not only today, but every day."

Prime Minister Tony Blair reads from the scripture "So faith, hope, love abide these three...." Do you remember your pax word? Do you hold it and keep it and use it so that it will give you access? Your pax word is not faith, for faith sustains you, reminds you, that you have access to this grace in which we stand. Your pax word is not hope, though it is the subject of our rejoicing as we find strength in the hope of sharing the glory of God. Do you remember your pax word? Can you speak it and live it? Jesus said, "If these were quiet even the stones would cry out." Are we to leave our Master alone with the stones to speak the pax word which he has given to us, which gives us access, freedom and power and courage and purpose? Faith, hope, and love and the greatest of these is love, and that is your pax word. Can you speak it and live it? Jesus wept over Jerusalem saying, "Would that even today you knew the things that make for peace!" Are we to leave him alone with the stones to speak, to weep over the places of our lives when we have the power of the access to the glory of God through our pax word, which he has given to us, which is love? Or will we enter our pax word: L - O - V - E?

Pleasing The Teacher

Ephesians 5:8-14

Pleasing the teacher. Paul writes to the Ephesians, "Try to learn what is pleasing to the Lord." Try to learn what is pleasing to the Good Shepherd, the Savior King, the Holy One, the Son of David, the Good Teacher/Rabbi. Sprinkled throughout the Gospels nearly seventy times, Jesus is referred to as rabbi or teacher. It is striking that in the garden as Mary encounters the risen Lord and he speaks her name, she responds, "Rab-eo'ni!" which means teacher. So Jesus, for many, was the good teacher, the good rabbi. And most of us gathered here know what it is to have a good teacher. Do you remember your favorite teacher? I have been fortunate to have more than a few.

It was spring quarter of his freshman year in college when John innocently wandered into a survey course on ancient civilization. The course was team-taught by a history professor and his graduate assistant. They considered the early cultures of Mesopotamia, Egypt, India, and China; the implications of early inventions and scientific thought — the wheel, the measurement of time, mathematics, and writing; the rise of the Greeks and Romans; and the emergence of world religions. John was not a person one would predict to get hooked on ancient history, but hooked he got. He began staying after class each lecture to ask additional questions, frequently walking with one of his professors back to the History Department office. Surely his energy for this subject was not due to an overly developed intellect. Instead, to this day, he remembers some very good teaching.

At the end of the term students were to submit the dreaded "Plutarch" paper. This was a critical treatment of some material penned by the ancient Greek author. John had done reasonably well on two mid-terms and with a moderately successful paper, he knew he would finish the course in good shape. As the class turned in the Plutarch paper, the professor asked the students to give him a few days and then stop by his office to pick up the graded papers. So, on a Friday afternoon John stopped by the History Department and after a few moments of pleasant conversation the professor said, "Well, I guess you want your paper ... They're right here in my drawer. I've got them arranged according to grade, the highest on top." With sweating palms, John watched him begin to thumb through a large pile of term papers. When he got through the first third without finding John's paper, John was getting nervous. When the professor got into the bottom third, John was sorry he had come. There were only a few papers left and then on the very bottom of the pile, John's paper. John was pale. Handing John his paper, with a twinkle in his eye the professor said, "You didn't think you could have gotten anything but an *A*, did you? The is the best paper of the term!" The richness of learning and the honest pursuit of knowledge were beginning to take root in this young life, and the professor's little joke pleasantly celebrated the work they had done together.

Do you have a favorite teacher? What makes a teacher good or great? Clearly, good teachers practice what they preach. They have deep insight and a passion for their subject. They have a knowledge and care for students. They are able to communicate material effectively and able to make concepts real, tangible, concrete, and important. They understand how people learn, and since they practice what they preach, they are excellent, committed practitioners, and they are active learners.

Many times in the Gospels, Jesus is known as teacher, good teacher, rabbi. What did Jesus teach?

> *Blessed are the poor in spirit, for theirs is the kingdom of heaven. Blessed are those who mourn, for they shall be comforted. Blessed are the meek, for they shall inherit*

the earth. Blessed are those who hunger and thirst for righteousness, for they shall be satisfied. Blessed are the merciful, for they shall obtain mercy. Blessed are the pure in heart, for they shall see God. Blessed are the peace-makers, for they shall be called sons of God. Blessed are those who are persecuted for righteousness' sake, for theirs is the kingdom of heaven. Blessed are you when men revile you and persecute you and utter all kinds of evil against you falsely on my account. Rejoice and be glad, for your reward is great in heaven, for so men persecuted the prophets who were before you.

— Matthew 5:3-12

Many have suggested that the summary of what Jesus taught is found in the Beatitudes as he speaks of the blessing which is to be found in meekness, humility, service, suffering, purity, and faithfulness. And it is safe to say he had deep insight and passion for his subject, and that he had knowledge of and care for his students.

But how did Jesus teach? We know much about how Jesus taught. He taught in parables. He was a weaver of word pictures. He helped understanding to become real, tangible, concrete, and important. He talked about the things his listeners would know about in their world. "You are the salt of the earth; but if salt has lost its taste, how shall its saltiness be restored? ... You are the light of the world. A city set on a hill cannot be hid. Nor do men light a lamp and put it under a bushel, but on a stand, and it gives light to all in the house" (Matthew 5:13-15). He spoke to his disciples of things which were known to them. "The kingdom of heaven is like a grain of mustard seed which a man took and sowed in his field. It is the smallest of all seeds ... The kingdom of heaven is like hidden treasure in a field which a man found and covered up. Then in his joy he goes and sells all that he has and buys that field. The kingdom of heaven is like a merchant in search of fine pearls, who on finding one of great value, went and sold all that he had and bought it" (Matthew 13, selected verses).

Jesus taught in parables and in ways people would understand. "There was a man going down from Jerusalem to Jericho, and he fell among robbers who stripped him and beat him and departed leaving him half dead ..." One in Jesus' hearing would know that the road to Jericho was a desolate and dangerous path. If one were to fall among robbers and be beaten and left for dead, one would pray for it not to happen on the Jericho road, for it was rugged and remote and timely help on this road would be unlikely to arrive.

Did Jesus ever use teaching aids? The children were coming to Jesus, that he might touch them, and the disciples rebuked them. But Jesus, when he saw it, was indignant and said to them, "Let the children come to me; do not hinder them, for to such belongs the kingdom of God." If Jesus was the good teacher, if he was the great teacher, and if he was able to reveal the mysteries of God even to children, then there may still be hope for ones like you and like me. And he placed a child on his knee and said, "Look at this child. Really, truly look at her. I say to you, whoever does not receive the kingdom of God like a child, shall not enter it" (Mark 10:13-15, author paraphrase).

Did Jesus use teaching aids? And at supper he took bread and after he had given thanks he broke it and gave it to them, saying, "This is my body which is given for you." And after supper he took the cup, saying, "This cup which is poured out for you is the new covenant in my blood" (Luke 22:19, 20).

And where did Jesus teach? In a boat at seaside, in Peter's home, in the synagogue, on the streets, on the hillside and the plain. He taught where the people could gather, where they would gather, and he offered them what a good teacher offers: deep insight with passion, word pictures, direction, guidance, and the best example of all — himself.

So how did the students behave? Usually well, but sometimes they were hungry. Sometimes Jesus needed to round them up something to eat. Sometimes they doubted or resisted what he said. The disciples often did not want to hear much about Jesus' suffering which was to come. Sometimes they came to bait him or to trap him. They asked, "Teacher, Moses wrote for us that if a man's brother's dies, having a wife but no children, the man must take the wife and raise up children for his brother. Now there were seven brothers; the first took a wife, and died without children; and the second and the third took her, and likewise all seven left no children and died. Afterward the woman also died. In the resurrection, therefore, whose wife will the woman be?" (Luke 20: 28-33).

"The scribes and the Pharisees brought a woman [to Jesus] who had been caught in the act of adultery. Placing her in the midst, they said to Jesus, 'Teacher, this woman has been caught in an act of adultery. Now the law of Moses commanded us to stone such. What do you say about her ...?' 'Let him who is without sin among you, be the first to throw a stone,' Jesus responded" (John 8: 3-7, author paraphrase).

But most of his disciples and his students heard him, learned from him, were given life by him, were enlivened by him, were nurtured in hope and saved by him.

How do you think Jesus felt about his teaching? When he spoke the Beatitudes on the hillside and when the parable of the Good Samaritan first came forth from his lips, how do you think Jesus felt about his teaching? And when he called forth disciples and they left everything to follow, to find life in him, how did he feel about his teaching? And when he entered Jerusalem with palm branches waving and garments carpeting his path, the enactment of God's king coming to enthronement, how did Jesus feel about his teaching? Or on that night when he took bread and broke it and offered a cup, or when he, with towel and basin, knelt to wash the disciples' feet, how did he feel about his teaching? Or when he prayed in the garden and his disciples could not stay awake with him, or on the cross when he said, "Father, father, why hast thou forsaken me?" how did he feel about his teaching? Or when in the garden of his resurrection, he spoke the name "Mary" and she said, "Rab-eo'ni," which means teacher, how did he feel about his teaching? Or when he said on the road to Damascus, "Saul, Saul why do you persecute me?" and Saul for a time was struck blind, but became Paul and became one of Christ's greatest students, an evangelist to the world, how did he feel about his teaching? And when he spoke your name and called you to be among his students and knew that you are a student, both willing and unwilling to do all which is required to live the lesson which he brings, and to do the teaching on his behalf which he requires, how did he feel about his teaching?

So it is interesting to think on whether Jesus' teaching was pleasing to him, to consider how he felt about his own teaching. And if we asked him, "How do you feel about your teaching, Jesus?" I expect he would sigh, "I'm not sure how I feel about my teaching. But I am interested in what you are learning ... and in what you are teaching for me."

If we are interested in pleasing this teacher, this good teacher, this rabbi, Rab-eo'ni , it will be by our *learning* and by our *teaching* that he will be pleased.

Have you ever had a favorite teacher? Maybe the One who sent you to *teach* on his behalf.

Pre-set Your Channel

Romans 8:6-11

How do I look? — I'm serious. How do I look? Do you think I glanced in the mirror to check before I walked out here to preach? Is my stole straight? Am I wearing socks that match?

Have you ever been somewhere and all of a sudden thought, "I wonder how I look?" A young woman walks into the bank on a cold day, pulls the hood from her head, scribbles some numbers onto a deposit form, and glances up to see the young man she has been hoping to date. "I wonder how I look," flashes through her mind. "Oh, I'm glad I wore lipstick this morning," she thinks. After a brief exchange, she does her banking, returns to her car, and sees reflected in the driver's door window a hairstyle flattened, messed up, crushed, collapsed. Instantly she condemns the coat hood which a moment ago had seemed so wonderfully warm.

How do I look? — Lately the lens on my camera has changed. I think it's become one of those panoramic, fisheye lenses. Every time it snaps a picture of me, I look wider.

Recently someone told me I look like David Letterman. We laughed and joked about how we wouldn't mind having all of the television money he makes. Later I thought, that's probably right, I do look like David Letterman, kind of. When I was in college there was a fellow on campus who looked astonishingly like me. I never met him but every time we passed on our way to class, I had to shake myself from the feeling that I was seeing my own reflection.

Standing some distance apart in the grocery checkout lanes are two professional colleagues. One is an attorney; the other is a judge fifteen years his senior. The attorney would like to remain in the good graces of this eminent and neatly dressed jurist. The unshaven lawyer has been painting his home all day, and is hoping to dash in and out of the grocery unseen to buy some pop for the neighbors who are helping him paint. Fortunately the lawyer sees the judge first and from a distance in time to duck down the aisle which sells sewing supplies.

Do I look like anyone to you? Some say I look like my dad and my sister. To my young sons I look like love, safety, shelter, entertainment, discipline, companionship, and a jungle gym. Humans and animals, early in life, develop a strong attachment to the appearance (even to the aroma) of certain individuals. We attach to our parents, siblings, and caregivers. We set our minds on them before we truly have the ability to think. We set our minds on them so deeply and so completely that our nature and life-long behavior are often molded into a similar pattern.

The recent film *Fly Away Home* tells a story which dramatically illustrates this "presetting" of the channel. Amy, a thirteen-year old New Zealander, goes to live with her father in Ontario, Canada, after her mother dies. It is a difficult reunion — Amy still grieving her mother and Tom, her father, unsure of how to be a dad.

When a nearby wetland is bulldozed by developers, Amy finds an abandoned Canada goose nest with eggs. After hatching the eggs in an incubator, the little goslings "imprint" on Amy, as if she is their mother and can teach them what they need to know about being geese.

But what will the geese do when it is time to migrate?

Tom and Amy fear that the geese may be *directionally challenged* — that they might get up in the air and not know which way is south. Father Tom comes up with a plan: Amy will fly an ultralight plane which the birds can follow to the Carolina coast. So as the story unfolds, the geese set their mind on Amy and Amy, on the geese, and Tom sets his mind on his daughter. Thus in the end, the geese, the father, and the daughter — fly away home.

And so to set the mind is an important matter. It can make all the difference in our search for the heart's true home. Paul writes, "To set the mind on the flesh is death, but to set the mind on the

Spirit is life and peace." Set the mind on Spirit — how can we do that?

Setting The Channel

If you buy a stereo you will undoubtedly go through a process called "channel pre-set." This simply makes it easy, at the touch of a finger, to tune in a specific, favorite channel. This has not always been true with radios. In the early days, most families had a "crystal radio set." The reception was poor, audio primitive, and tuning tricky. One would strain to hear the voice of Arthur Godfrey or Bing Crosby or Edward R. Murrow. And when a channel was found, clearly transmitting and well received, one spent some time listening to the program to see what was being presented before moving on to another. Not so today. An additional feature on modern audio sets is called "channel scan." Press this button and the radio will quickly move through all available channels, pausing two or three seconds at each. One must hurriedly press another button to stop the scanning and choose a station. In television, a similar phenomenon is called channel surfing, where a person with a remote quickly flips through all of the channels to see if "anything's on." How convenient it is in selecting entertainment — rapid scanning, channel surfing — and how dangerous it is in selecting a Savior.

Paul instructs Christians that to set the mind on flesh is death. And we know what he means. There are many signals we receive attempting to tell us what is important, what is beautiful, what is good, what is helpful, what is ultimately of worth. If we indiscriminately listen to these many voices, we will become confused, mired, distracted, and agitated by the constant cacophony. To come upon a person in such a state is as if we were present when Jesus encountered the man with an unclean spirit whose name was Legion, "for they were many." And Jesus cast out the unclean spirits which entered a herd of swine, and numbered about two thousand (Mark 5: 2-13).

Sometimes we feel as if we are the ones so bombarded by voices of unclean spirits, on the verge of entering us to claim us, that we long for the One Voice of God to send a signal clear and strong overcoming all others. A pastor recently commented on the radio broadcast of his Sunday service. "No matter how strong our signal," he said, "there is always someone at the edge of our broadcast area. They call and speak of 'straining to hear, of static, of frustration.' I feel helpless when I receive such a call, but lately I've changed the way I respond. I say, 'I'm glad you want to hear our broadcast and I'm thankful for that. And when it isn't clearly received, you feel helpless and frustrated. That's always the way it is at the edge of the signal. But there are two things we can do when we are truly trying to hear: 1) we can hope that the signal from the sender will get stronger or 2) we can move closer to the source.' "

When I Don't Recognize Myself

I have to admit there are times when I don't want to know how I look. Sometimes someone will say, "You look tired!" or "Are you feeling okay?" after which, if I was feeling just fine, I don't.

It is not uncommon in marriages, amidst the pressures of daily living, for one partner to blurt out to the other, "I'm not sure I know you anymore!" And then, if they are wise, husband and wife, wife and husband, go through a season of reconnecting.

And it is also somewhat common to feel that way even when we look in the mirror. "I'm not sure I know you anymore." This feeling especially comes after we have blown up at a loved one or friend, or in a time when we have neglected those things which are truly of greatest importance to us in favor of immediate demands of lesser importance.

Not recognizing ourselves is often the case when we compare who we are with who we thought we would be, who we set out to be, or who we hoped we would be. "When I am a parent, I will *never* say that to my child!" I thought after hearing my dad say, "Because I said so," for the umpteenth time. This morning in frustration and confusion I said, "Because I said so!" to my child. Who was it that sent those words flying into his bedroom? — I didn't recognize him.

Peter declared to Jesus, "Though they all fall away ... I will never fall away."

Jesus said to him, "Truly, I say to you, this very night, before the cock crows, you will deny me three times."

Peter said to Jesus, "Even if I must die with you, I will not deny you" (Matthew 26:33-35). Peter knew who he hoped to be, but Jesus knew better.

So how do I look — spiritually? Do you recognize me; do I recognize myself — spiritually? Do I look like anyone to you, spiritually? To set your mind on flesh is death, but to set your mind on Spirit is life and peace. God dwells in you and says, "You look like me." God is the sender, you are the receiver. God is the Source of the signal, you are the one tuned to the signal. If the signal comes and goes, is at times strongly present but then fades away, we can do one of two things. We can always hope the signal will get stronger, living with the frustration of its coming and going, living with static and interference and competing signals, or we can move closer to the Source; we can pre-set to the Spirit of life and peace. We can position ourselves to hear the signal, strong and sure. Jesus said, "My sheep hear my voice, and I know them, and they follow me; and I give them eternal life, and they never perish, and no one shall snatch them out of my hand" (John 10:27-28). I guess I really don't recognize myself. I am different than I was before, writes Paul. I have become a new person because I have heard his voice.

Pre-set your channel to his voice. Come close to the Source. And you will find comfort and strength for the living of these days. Amen.

The Holy Vessel
Is Empty

Philippians 2:5-11

It was the early 1400s and France was without a king. The one who could be king was such a spindly, weak-limbed, weak-willed presence that French and English soldiers, mercenaries, and criminals fought constantly for control of France. Into this power vacuum stepped a teenage girl who had heard (by her description) "a worthy voice" which she took to be a messenger from God, and saw a great light. "You must go to the aid of your king," the voice directed her. And so Joan of Arc went forth, determined and courageous. She led soldiers by the thousands and, though wounded, continued to pursue the interests of France and her king until Charles the VII was crowned.

On May 23, 1430, Joan of Arc was captured in battle, turned over to the English, and tried by a conspiratorial church for heresy because the voices, the church claimed, were the messengers of Satan. She was convicted and placed in the hands of secular authorities for execution. On May 30, 1431, Joan was burned at the stake — holding fast to her claim, "Everything good I have done, I have done at the command of my voices." Joan of Arc, teenage peasant, woman warrior, servant of France, passed from this earth aged nineteen years.[1]

Palm Sunday is a time when we remember the triumphal entry of Jesus into Jerusalem. Jesus riding on a colt, palm branches waving, garments carpeting his path, the kind of a welcome that was reserved for a hero king returning from a successful military campaign, or reserved for the enthronement of God's chosen king of Israel. So here is Jesus in the midst of great enthusiasm,

45

"Hosanna! Blessed is the one who comes in the name of the Lord!" and because of the tumult, the scribes and the Pharisees are agitated. "Rebuke your disciples!" they say to Jesus. But Jesus responds, "If these were silent, the very stones would cry out" (Luke 19:38-40). And cry out they will, for within days these who are following him in joy and celebration will run away and will fall into hiding. For this Sunday is also called Passion Sunday, which initiates the week of Christ's Passion — the time when we remember how he poured himself out for us to save us. Paul writes in Philippians, "Have this mind among yourselves, which is yours in Christ Jesus, who, though he was in the form of God, did not count equality with God a thing to be grasped, but emptied himself, taking the form of a servant, being born in the likeness of men. And being found in human form he humbled himself and became obedient unto death, even death on a cross" (Philippians 2:5-8). This entry into Jerusalem marks the setting into motion events which will bring to completion Christ's self-emptying. And before we meet again for our weekly Sunday worship celebration, we will hear Christ say, "It is finished," which is to say, the Holy Vessel is empty.

For many, *purposeful self-emptying* has a sacred quality to it. Some suggest the self-emptying of Joan of Arc has such a quality, or of Ghandi, or Martin Luther King, Jr.

And it is because in most circumstances we seek to do exactly the opposite — to be full rather than empty — that the act of self-emptying has such power when embraced with intention and calm resolve.

Some things in our lives and in our world are not meant to be empty. Churches are to be filled with worshipers, schools with students, hospitals with patients, streets with travelers, parks with picnickers, concert halls with musicians. Or to think in another way — growing fields are to be filled with crops. And speaking anatomically, the circulatory system with something to circulate.

Refrigerator shelves are to be filled with food, the heart to be filled with love, and the community filled with hope. Some things are not meant to be empty. Great migrations of humankind have occurred because of emptiness. If the stomach is empty or is likely

46

to be, by the hundreds of thousands people migrate in search of food.

It was the fear of empty stomachs that sent Elim-elech and his wife Naomi from Judah to Moab with their two sons. While in Moab the sons married Orpah and Ruth. After Elim-elech had passed from this earth, both sons also died, leaving Naomi with her daughters-in-law Orpah and Ruth. After having heard that things had gotten better in Judah, Naomi started with her daughters-in-law for home, but then she told them, "Go, return each of you to your mother's house. And may the Lord deal kindly with you...." Orpah left Naomi to return to her mother's home, but Ruth clung to Naomi saying, "Entreat me not to leave you or to return from following you; for where you go I will go, and where you lodge I will lodge; your people shall be my people and your God my God; where you die I will die, and there I will be buried...." And so the two returned to Judah, to Bethlehem, and the town was stirred because of them, saying, "Is this Naomi?" "Do not call me Naomi," she said to them. "Call me Mara, for the Almighty has dealt bitterly with me. I went away full, and the Lord has brought me back empty" (Ruth 1, selected verses). Some things are not meant to be empty. Homes are not meant to be empty, hearts are meant to be filled with love, and the future, with promise. So, we pause in wonderment as Ruth proclaims her love for Naomi, risking her own security and pledging to remain with Naomi on this life journey. Purposeful self-emptying has a sacred quality to it. Some suggest that the self-emptying of Ruth has such a quality.

When Empty Is Good

Sometimes empty is good. A dock is empty because a ship has been launched, and a womb is empty when a babe has been born. A hotel room is empty and a traveler finds welcomed rest. A loaf of bread is broken and shared; a cup is passed and is emptied. This empty is good.

Jesus was asked to come for supper to the home of a Pharisee, not surprisingly because though some of the Pharisees gave Jesus trouble not all of them did. Some Pharisees, like Nicodemus, were his friends. Now after Jesus had taken his place at the table, a woman of the city, a sinner, brought an alabaster flask of fine ointment, and weeping, she began to wet his feet with her tears and wipe them with her hair. She kissed his feet and anointed them with the ointment.

Jesus' host, the Pharisee, said to himself, "If Jesus were truly a prophet, he would have known what sort of woman this is who is touching him."

And Jesus said to his host, "Simon, I have something to say to you."

"What is it, Teacher?" he asked.

And Jesus said, "A certain creditor had two debtors; one owed five hundred denarii, and the other fifty. When they could not pay, he forgave them both. Now which of them will love him more?"

Simon answered, "The one, I suppose, to whom he forgave more." And Jesus said to him, "You have judged rightly."

Then turning toward the woman he continued, "Do you see this woman? I entered your house, you gave me no water for my feet, but she has wet my feet with her tears and wiped them with her hair. You gave me no kiss, but from the time I came in she has not ceased to kiss my feet. You did not anoint my head with oil, but she has anointed my feet with ointment. Therefore I tell you, her sins, which are many, are forgiven, for she loved much...."

And Jesus said to her, "Your sins are forgiven" (Luke 7:36-48, author paraphrase).

Empty is good when an alabaster flask is broken to anoint the feet of the Savior. Empty is good when our reservoir of sin is poured out because by him our sins are forgiven.

And so Jesus, triumphant, enters Jerusalem and sets in motion events which bring to completion his self-emptying.

Jesus did not cling to his divine power but emptied himself and became as we are; he became more than we are. In a week's time he transforms from celebrated leader to bound prisoner. He is scourged, humiliated, and led to a cross where his self-emptying is made complete.

On this Palm Sunday, on this Passion Sunday, it would be well if we likewise embark upon a pathway which will lead to self-emptying, following the example of many who have come before, some of whom have lived in our midst and even in our homes. Break your alabaster flask and empty the ointment. Bring your storehouse of treasure, of human power and passion, release your over-confident self-reliance and your over-powering worry for tomorrow. Empty yourself, empty yourself, empty yourself, and when your holy vessel, when the vessel of your own God-given life is empty, as someone has written, you will be transformed from the need to control, from the desire always to have it your own way, from the need to be out front at the head of the procession, from the need to lead; you will be transformed in the joy of being led by God, by Christ, by the Spirit.[2]

"Have this mind among yourselves, which is yours in Christ Jesus, who, though he was in the form of God, did not count equality with God a thing to be grasped, but emptied himself, taking the form of a servant ..." (Philippians 2:5-7).

And when your holy vessel is empty, you will be transformed in the joy of being lead by God, by Christ, by the Spirit. Father, into your hands we commend our emptiness, and we trust your hand will lead.

---

1. Beth Randall, "Illuminating Lives: Joan of Arc," copyright 1996, www.mcs.drexel.edu/~gbrandal/Illum_html/Joan.html

2. Henri Nouwen, *In the Name of Jesus* (New York: The Crossroad Publishing Company, 1989), p. 61.

Say: "I Remember"

1 Corinthians 11:23-26

How good are you at remembering? Do you remember when you got your driver's license and who taught you to drive? Do you remember your first day of school, your pets, all the pets you ever had? What were their names? Did you ever have a bug as a pet? Where did you go on your first date? What was your first job? How good are you at remembering? Did your parents have siblings? What were their names? How about your grandparents, your great-grandparents? This evening we break this bread and take this cup because Jesus said, "Do this in remembrance of me." How good are you at remembering?

Two fellows got together recently who had not seen each other for years. After a warm greeting, the conversation turned to the "good old days" and a discussion of their second grade teacher.

"Do you remember Mrs. Holland? Do you remember what a thing she had for flash cards?"

"I sure do. I always thought I was pretty good at addition and multiplication but that darn ... what was his name? That kid that was so good at flash cards."

"Oh, I know who you mean, let me think ... Carl Fox, yeah, Carl Fox. You know what I heard about him?"

"What?"

"I heard he went to MIT. Studied geophysics. He's been all over the world lookin' for oil."

How good are you at remembering? In 1948 *I Remember Mama* was a hit film. Set in San Francisco around 1900, a middle class Norwegian immigrant family is held together by an untiring,

51

resourceful, stern but loving matriarch played by Irene Dunn. The life of the family is recalled in flash-back style as one of the daughters, Katrine, reads from her diary. She narrates: "But first and foremost, I remember Mama."

How good are you at remembering? Is there someone in your family from whom your compass finds its direction? An aunt or an uncle, a parent, a grandparent? Or someone outside the family circle who bestowed a special kindness: the one who spent extra time teaching you to read? Or the one who took you on all those fishing trips? Is it the one from whom you learned to sew, or to paint, or to plant a garden? And, oh, how challenging it is when the memory begins to fade. "My mind's just not as quick as it used to be." "I can remember things way back, but don't ask me a lot about what happened this week." "I went to visit Mom today, but I'm not sure she knew it was me." How is your remembering?

Do you remember the One we have gathered to remember this evening? How Simeon simply catching a glimpse of him felt his life complete? Do you remember how he called James and John and Andrew and Peter, called Matthew and Bartholomew and Judas? How he went from place to place and would eat with anyone? Do you remember how he made the lame to walk and gave speech to those who could not speak, sight to those who could not see? Do you remember how tired he got, how we all leaned on him and how he occasionally forgot even to eat? Do you remember that day on the hillside when he turned to us, when there were so many and he said, "You give them something to eat." And we could not. But he took the bread and the fish and he fed them. Do you remember how he wept when Lazarus died because they were friends? They really were good friends. And what he said at Lazarus' tomb? We really didn't want to open it because of the stench. He had been dead for quite some time. But he said, "Lazarus, come forth." And we couldn't believe it. He did come forth and we were so amazed he had to tell us to unwrap the burial shroud.

And how the children loved him. I think that is why he enjoyed his ride on that colt into Jerusalem. The children so enjoyed it, waving branches and singing. Everyone did.

On the last night, he was tired and he wanted to be remembered. He knew that the storm clouds of destruction were gathering and that even one of his own would be conspiring against him. And he knew his great agony would come and he wanted everyone at that table to know what great love he had for them. Don't forget my love for you. This is my body broken. This is the cup of the new covenant in my blood. It is because of my love for you that I do this. When you break the bread and when you take the cup say: "I remember."

People of God, we remember. As you take this bread and receive the cup poured out, say: " I remember. I remember who you are and what you did. And I will *never* forget." Amen.

The Day God Forgot

Hewbrews 10:16-25

Two boys are racing their bicycles. Spring has sprung and they feel the gentle warmth of late afternoon rushing past their ears as they barrel down the street. Just in front of them are two home-made ramps, and beyond the ramps, a finish line. They're both standing now to exert a little more force on the pedals. Gracefully into the air flies one, as the other begins to rotate slightly. Landing straight and pushing onto the finish line is only one of the riders. The other lands, bounces, flips, groans, the right arm bending where one should not have a bend. Immediately tears. A friend peering down, neighbors gathering, "O God, why did this have to happen to me!" he exclaims as he is being loaded up for a trip to the emergency room. Six weeks in a cast and greater caution on his bicycle mark the rest of his summer.

O God, Why Did This Have To Happen?

In so many ways "O God, why did this have to happen?" comes into our minds and into our lives. Even on this day when we remember that Jesus prayed, "If it be Thy will, let this cup pass from me ..." and that the cup did not pass from him; instead he drank from it deeply. So, we come to the day God forgot. "My God, my God, why have you forsaken me?" Why have you forgotten me? — And we know how he feels. In our world and in our lives we have all too many times when we think, "This cannot be happening."

A team of teenage rugby players crashes in the Andes Mountains and must survive for over seventy days, far above the tree line on a glacier, huddled together in their broken craft while some of their comrades perish. "This cannot be happening."

Brown shirts from the fanatical followers of the new German chancellor burn Jewish synagogues and ransack and loot Jewish businesses all in the night. *Kristallnacht* as it will be known: the night of broken glass. Dachau and Buchenwald follow. "This cannot be happening."

Idi Amin comes to power in Uganda and many atrocities follow. "This cannot be happening."

Some believe that the federal government is a threat to our liberty and is moving toward oppressive authority; an evil conspiracy and the Alfred P. Murrah Federal Building in Oklahoma City is destroyed along with 168 lives. "This cannot be happening."

Lt. William Calley, tired, sick, and twisted by horrors of war, turns his military might on innocent civilians, and only later we learn of the village named My Lai halfway around the globe. "This cannot be happening."

We go to a family doctor for a routine check-up and there is a spot on our lung, further tests are needed. "This cannot be happening."

Our children, who have so blissfully wed just four years ago, now find pain in being together and are considering whether their future would be better spent apart. "This cannot be happening."

Our friends whom we enjoy so much and who make us feel at home and welcome and worthwhile in our new high school are into some things we don't believe are right. It's clear if we don't go along, we won't be part of the group. "This cannot be happening."

Jesus was barely born when Herod came calling. Herod searched for the newborn babe and, seeking to do him harm, eliminated every baby boy in the community who could have possibly been him — the *Slaughter of the Innocents.* "This cannot be happening."

He Descended Into Hell

"I believe in God the Father Almighty, maker of heaven and earth; and in Jesus Christ his only Son our Lord: who was conceived

56

by the Holy Spirit, born of the Virgin Mary, suffered under Pontius Pilate, was crucified, dead, and buried; he descended into hell ..." (The Apostles' Creed).

A traditional belief of the church is that Christ descended into hell and a part of the hell he descended into must have been the solitary hell of being alone as he was arrested, alone as he was tried, alone as he was beaten, and isolated alone on the cross. Left to his pain, left to his doubts, left to his anguish. "My God, my God, why hast thou forsaken me?" And so we ask why did this have to happen? Whenever we encounter what seems to be a day God forgot, we ask, "Why did this have to happen"? Simply put, the answer almost always is, "It didn't have to happen." God does not cause these painful things to happen nor does God create extreme pain and difficulty to teach us. But what does need to happen, and what is the salvific momentum of Christ's faithfulness on the cross, is that he stayed true to God, even in the midst of this excruciating conclusion of his human experience. He felt what we feel, he was tempted as we are tempted, he hurt as we hurt, and he wept as we weep; and yet he stayed true to God in ways that we are inspired by, taught by, claimed by, saved by. So on that Friday, which was bad before it was good, God forgot not about Jesus, not about His love for His son, not about those who had followed him, not about the world He loves, but rather God forgot something else. In Hebrews we read, "This is the covenant that I will make with them after those days, says the Lord: I will put my laws on their hearts, and write them on their minds," then he adds, "I will remember their sins and their misdeeds no more" (Hebrews 10:16-17). This is the day God forgot, but God didn't forget Jesus, not the ones who followed him, not the world he loves, not you and not me. This is the day God forgot our sins and our misdeeds and embraced us with a new love made manifest in our Lord as he suffered and died. His love poured out that we might be new persons in his love.

O God, why is this happening to me? This great love which you have given, this great sacrifice which you have made, this great forgetting which you have done, this great wiping clean of the slate which you have accomplished, why is this happening to us? It is happening so that you might know the way, the truth, and the life, that you might have abundance in your living, that you might live after the example of Jesus with a special quality in your life and love. We the church, because God forgot, must be the forgiving fellowship of the forgiven; we must be the reconciling *koinonia* of the reconciled. In this way we are the first fruits of the kingdom and become, as Desmond Tutu suggests, "a *verbum visible*, a kind of audio-visual aid for the sake of the world."[1] O God, why is this happening to me? I know not why except for the unfathomable mystery of your love. Thank you for forgetting. Thank you for Jesus. Thank you for love poured out. Amen.

---

1. Desmond M. Tutu, "Allies of God," *Weavings*, Vol. 5, Number 1, (January/February 1990), p. 41.

Sermon Series:
Easter: A Time For Higher Things

Introduction

Easter is *the* glorious time in the Christian year. God's victory is proclaimed through Word and song and Christians everywhere are encouraged to go into the world with renewed confidence and courage to pick up the ministry of the Risen Christ.

And it is in part because of our response to Easter that I find the predawn scene in the garden of Christ's resurrection as reported in the Gospel of Matthew so intriguing. Early, the two Marys go to see the sepulchre and there is a great earthquake. This apparently has something to do with the fact that an angel of the Lord has rolled back the stone and then sits down upon it. The angel, at least to the hardened Roman guards, is fearful enough in appearance to make them "tremble and become like dead men" (Matthew 28:4). But to the women the angel says, "Don't be afraid, I know you seek Jesus...."

And that is the challenge for us as God's children of Easter, "Don't be afraid while you seek Jesus." We are called to live as new people in the midst of tests and trials, in challenge and sacrifice, all the while listening for an echo of rejoicing which rings still in the heavens because of what God has done and is doing. And then we are called to add to that song our voices. I think this was the angel's plan all along, for if we are singing we are less likely to be afraid.

Easter is a time for higher things. Easter is also a time for other things, for earthquakes and for guards scared out of their wits, for humble women coming to care for the body of their beloved Lord. Easter is a time for God and a time for us; it is a time for singing, lest we might otherwise be afraid. In these sermons I hope you hear an echo of rejoicing and I hope in some way they will help you join that song.

Easter: A Time For Higher Things

Colossians 3:1-4

Christ the Lord is risen today, Alleluia!

"If then you have been raised with Christ, seek the things that are above, where Christ is, seated at the right hand of God. Set your mind on things that are above ..." (Colossians 3:1-2a). And we, today, come to set our minds on things that are above. We come to hear the Hallelujah Chorus, and to worship in the aroma of lilies. We come to hear life proclaimed victorious over death and that Christ our Lord will live forevermore. We have come seeking higher things, putting behind us, at least for the moment, things which are not life-enhancing, life-sustaining, life-generating. We leave behind the grays and dark things which grab, consume, destroy, and diminish. At least for this shining moment we come to witness the dawning of God's promised kingdom and to hear words which ring with a beautiful resonance in the cathedral of the soul.

We come because we want to climb the mountain; we want to breathe the clear air and to see with the long view which reaches to the threshold of eternity. We come again to experience the adventure of having held the hand of God and to allow our vision to be directed to higher things which only those who know God can see.

It is like when John Glenn, that ancient astronaut, announced that he would again return to space. He said 36 years after his first orbital flight, "I see this as another adventure into the unknown."[1] We come today because we seek another adventure — not into the unknown but into the known; into that which has been made known to us as truer than true, as God's revelation to all of humankind who will seek to hear and understand it. We come this day wanting to hear the Alleluias, wanting to smell the lilies, wanting to climb the mountain once again, wanting to have another adventure, not into the unknown but into the known which has been revealed to us as truer than true, as life over death, as victory proclaimed, as the realm of God made manifest even in this time and in this place.

Yet if we are to understand the higher things which God has in store for us, we must take again the journey to the garden tomb with Mary. We must walk with her in the shadows, as she did in the early morning, while it was still dark, and discovered that the stone had been rolled away. It was still in the black of night when she barely saw that the stone had been disturbed, and she was disturbed by it. So she went running to Simon Peter and the other disciple, reporting through her tears, "They have taken the Lord out of the tomb and we do not know where they have laid him." Who knows whether or not Peter and the disciple had even awakened from sleep. But shaken to maximum attention they came running to the tomb. When they arrived where the stone had been disturbed, they were disturbed by it and stooped to look in.

If we are to understand the higher things which God has in store for us today, then we must also stoop to look into the place where the body had lain. We must travel with Mary and Peter and the other unnamed disciple to the place where the stone has been disturbed and be disturbed ourselves by it. We must go to the place of shadow, darkness, and death, not only in this story but also in our own story, where light has yet to conquer the darkness, where shadows still roam, where stone doorways have yet to be opened, and where it would be disturbing to us if they were opened. And we know that God will disturb those stone doorways as well; the doorways which, if opened, will reveal much about ourselves. And if we go there, we are uncertain we will even be able to love ourselves, and we might wonder if, in those dark places, God will be able to love us. But we must go to those places to understand that the ones who placed Christ in the tomb, those who sought to lock him up there, were convinced that the news he did bring, the gospel he did preach, was simply more good than this world can stand.

We must go to those places because it is only by going there that we will understand the higher things God is calling us to understand today: that God's love and God's light is greater than any darkness we fear in our world or even in ourselves. We must go to those places because, by going to the place of shadow, we can understand the coming of the light, by going to the valley we find comfort as we stand with Jesus on the hillside. So if on this day we are to come with God to the heights and to ponder higher things pleasantly, then we must also walk with Mary in the garden of darkness where the stone has been disturbed and where she has been disturbed by it.

Early in this century there was one who knew more than a little about the heights. Auguste Piccard, a Swiss-born physicist, became best known for his design of a pressurized balloon gondola, and its successful use in high altitude operation. The aluminum spherical gondola in the years 1931 and 1932 made two record-setting high altitude flights, the second carrying Piccard to the altitude of nearly ten miles above sea level. His achievements were spectacular and contributed greatly to the international body of knowledge, which eventually led to putting humans safely in space. But reaching the heights was not enough for Auguste Piccard. A decade passed and he was again at work on a new project, a new feat of exploration — physics and engineering. Auguste Piccard was creating a bathyscaphe — a diving bell designed to support human passengers in the extreme depths of the ocean. In 1953, when Piccard was aged 69 years, he piloted his bathyscaphe to 10,330 feet below the ocean's surface, the greatest depth humans had ever attained. His son, Jacques, less than a year after his father's death in 1963, piloted a similar craft to the deepest point on earth — 35,800 feet, nearly seven miles beneath the waves.[2]

To understand the heights we must know the depths. If we meet God on the mountain we will also meet him in the valley.

The Lord is my shepherd, I shall not want; he makes me lie down in green pastures. He leads me beside still waters; he restores my soul. He leads me in the paths of righteousness for his name's sake. **Even though I walk**

through the valley of the shadow of death, I fear no evil;
For thou art with me....   — Psalm 23:1-4

If we are to meet God in the mystery of the mountain, to be held by Him in the heights, then we must also marvel with Mary that the stone has been disturbed, and with the disciples, stoop to look in the place of shadow and darkness, a place we fear we will find only death.

In 1841 an ordained medical missionary began his work along the Zambezi River in Africa. In that time the geography of Africa was unknown to westerners. Maps showed the edges of the continent but the interior was left blank. Dr. David Livingstone began his thirty-year exploration and service of God and humankind in this unknown region. He traveled the continent, suffering illness and injury, becoming acquainted with indigenous people and winning their welcome, charting new courses, encountering slave traders, buying slaves and setting them free, all in the name of God and of God's church. If the fruit of his work was measured in souls saved, it would have been insignificant. But measured by the intensity of his service, the magnitude of his sacrifice, and the enormity of what he added to world knowledge and understanding of an unknown wilderness, it is not hard to understand why, when Livingstone at age sixty succumbed to illness deep in the African forest, it is said that all Britain wept when his body was returned home for burial. His tombstone reads: BROUGHT BY FAITHFUL HAND OVER LAND AND SEA, DAVID LIVINGSTONE: MISSIONARY, TRAVELER, PHILANTHROPIST. FOR THIRTY YEARS HIS LIFE WAS SPENT IN AN UNWEARIED EFFORT TO EVANGELIZE THE NATIVE RACES, TO EXPLORE THE UNDISCOVERED SECRETS AND ABOLISH THE SLAVE TRADE.

On one 1700-mile journey along the Zambezi River, David Livingstone traveled from the equatorial jungle of Angola and the Republic of the Congo through the middle of the continent, through the Rift Valley as it thunders and falls down canyons deeper than our Grand Canyon until it reaches its opening at the Indian Ocean. It was on this trip that David Livingstone became the first European to reach Victoria Falls. The spectacular waterfall is twice as deep and twice as wide as Niagra Falls. Because of the tremendous roar and the ever-present veil of mist, the indigenous Kalolo-Lozi people dubbed the falls Mosi-oa-tunya ("The Smoke that Thunders").[3] Of his most awe-inspiring discovery he later wrote: "Victoria Falls must have been gazed upon by angels in their flight." David Livingstone knew that to experience higher things for him meant to spend his life in the darkness and shadows of the jungle.[4]

And so, dear friends, as we come here today seeking to hear the Hallelujah Chorus and worship in the aroma of lilies, as we seek to place our hand in God's hand and to consider higher things, let us, as this moment concludes and as we move on to other responsibilities, tasks, and turmoil, even into the valley — let us remember what we have seen here, what we have heard in this place, the claim which has been made. What we have seen here together reminds us of the truth of God which is over all that is. On that day long ago, God came to a place of death and disturbed the stone. And God today and every day comes to the garden of shadow and darkness and death and disturbs the stone. He calls us forth to life. Let us remember what we have seen here, what we have heard here, what we have sung here, what we have spoken here — that God disturbs the stone, does not leave that stone unturned. Then unspectacularly, and with the regularity of tomorrow, let us with Georgia Harkness recite:

> The vision fades; the Easter joy is past.
> Again in dull drab paths our lot is cast.
> The heavens no longer sing, the war clouds lower.
> O Lord, where art thou in thy risen power?
> The calm voice speaks — it answers all I ask.
> "I am beside you in the daily task."[5]

Easter is a time for higher things and may God Easter in us in all of our days and in all of our places, in the valley and on the hillside. And as we go forth we should expect that in the high places and in the valleys, even if we come to a canyon of calamity, on the mountain and in the really rough places, we will find, in one as in the other, surprisingly and powerfully, a Victoria Falls of Grace raining down upon us, washing over us, bathing us with a sense of having been saved, of having been claimed, of having been blessed; bathing us with a sense of the One who makes us whole and who we proclaim this day victorious. Thanks be to God for Easter — a time for higher and deeper things.

---

1. Jeffrey Kluger, "The Right Stuff, 36 Years Later," *Time,* Vol. 151 No. 3, Jan. 26, 1998, p. 58.

2. "Piccard, Auguste," *Encyclopedia Britanica,* 1993 edition, Vol. 9, p. 422.

3. "Victoria Falls," *Encyclopedia Britanica,* 1993 edition, Vol. 12, p. 352.

4. Alvin Austin, "Discovering Livingstone: the Man, the Missionary, the Explorer, the Legend," *Christian History,* Vol. XVI, No. 4, Fall 1997, p. 10.

5. Georgia Harkness, *The Living Pulpit,* Vol. 7, No. 1, January/March 1998, p. 32.

A Time Of Tests, Trials, And An Echo Of Rejoicing

1 Peter 1:3-9

I don't test well. I know the material, but I'm not sure I gave that impression on the test. I'm not a good test taker.

I took the college entrance exam preparation course, and one thing you *have* to be able to do on *this* test is make a good guess. I didn't know the material, but I did great on the test. — Go figure.

A young man comes into class and seats himself in his normal place. He has studied all night. He does not like to prepare for a test in this way, but he wanted to make sure he had command of all of the material — and now he is ready. In ninety minutes the final will be over, and he will be headed back to his dorm for some serious sleep. He is an auditory learner, so as usual, he had great lecture notes, but this time he also went carefully over *all* of the assigned reading. It is to be an essay test. The professor distributes the blue books. "Inside your blue books you will find three questions," he states. "Answer all three. Use your time wisely and be thorough."

The young man opens the blue book and reviews the questions, concluding that they are challenging but do-able. He gets out his pencil and starts to write. Next to him is seated a fellow with a bad cold. Instead of pulling out a pencil, he pulls out Kleenex in a plastic package. He blows, sniffs, and wipes as he reads the questions. Then comes a loud, juicy sneeze. For the next several minutes he gives up on his nose and breathes loudly through his mouth. Then a second package of Kleenex noisily opened, then another sneeze....

The original young man has now placed a finger in one ear and adjusted the angle of his chair pointing it slightly away from the fellow with the cold. It is twenty minutes into the final and he realizes he has hardly written anything — he feels as though he has lost his ability to think.

Have you ever been tested? In First Peter we read that our faith, which is as precious as gold, will be tested by fire.

And of course Jesus was tested. The Scribes, Pharisees, and Sad'ducees used to come around to test him, trying to trip him up, like reporters at a White House press briefing, attempting to ask that one carefully prepared question which would finally stump the Master.

> *Then the Pharisees went and took counsel how to entangle him in his talk. And they sent their disciples to him, along with the Hero'di-ans, saying, "Teacher, we know that you are true, and teach the way of God truthfully, and care for no man; for you do not regard the position of men. Tell us, then, what you think. Is it lawful to pay taxes to Caesar, or not?"* — Matthew 22:15-17

And later ...

> *The same day Sad'ducees came to him, who say that there is no resurrection; and they asked him a question, saying, "Teacher, Moses said, 'If a man dies, having no children, his brother must marry the widow, and raise up children for his brother.' Now there were seven brothers among us; the first married, and died, and having no children left his wife to his brother. So too the second and third, down to the seventh. After them all, the woman died. In the resurrection, therefore, to which of the seven will she be wife? For they all had her."* — Matthew 22:23-28

Interesting questions. Interesting *questioners.*

But Jesus was more greatly tested by disciples who did not understand his teaching, by synagogue officials who would not receive his gospel, by the people who came seeking only signs and wonders. And he was tested by the anguish of arrest and trial, worldly power for a time eclipsing the heavenly Light; he was tested by pain and punishment for crimes uncommitted.

And others, of course, followed. Stephen was stoned; James was beheaded; Peter and Paul were executed; Simeon, cousin of Jesus, Bishop of Jerusalem, was killed. And how many more throughout Christian history have faced tests and trials? Have you?

In First Peter we read that our faith, which is as precious as gold, will be tested by fire.

> *In this you rejoice, though now for a little while you may have to suffer various trials, so that the genuineness of your faith, more precious than gold which though perishable is tested by fire, may redound to praise and glory and honor at the revelation of Jesus Christ.*
> — *1 Peter 1:6-7*

So this letter which was written to Christians in the midst of severe persecution proclaims: "*In this you rejoice ... so that the genuineness of your faith ... may redound to praise and glory and honor at the revelation of Jesus Christ.*" Rejoice, in the midst of my trials? In the midst of my testing? What kind of advice is that?!

Have you ever wondered what Jesus was looking for when he invited his disciples to come along? Do you suppose it was the ability to test well?

No Fear Of The Test

On October 14, 1947, at an isolated airstrip in the Mojave Desert a group of pilots gathered in a hangar with a sense that history was to be made that day. One of them was Chuck Yeager — decorated World War II pilot and the one selected to fly the X-1 rocket plane in an attempt to fly faster than the speed of sound. In earlier tests, planes approaching Mach 1 experienced such terrible vibration and buffeting that pilots found it virtually impossible to retain control of the craft. As Yeager boarded the X-1 for the attempt, though he knew his plane well and earlier flights had taken him close to Mach

1, he still felt like he was flying into the unknown. But one thing is sure: he was not afraid of the test.[1]

A Question Of Character

When Branch Rickey set out to break the color barrrier in professional baseball, he searched for a black player who would be able to face the tests and trials ahead of him: the taunts and troubles, the abuse and isolation, the public attention and microscopic scrutiny. He found such a person in Jackie Robinson.

Likewise when the Freedom Riders rode Greyhound buses into the United States' segregated South, they were trained to face tests and trials, to receive violence but not to return violence. They were schooled in civil disobedience and they were selected based on character in order to ensure their ability to put the best face on the trials which surely would come.

So it was with Jesus as he looked for his disciples, as he sought those who would follow him, who could follow him in the face of tests and trials which undoubtedly would come, as he sought disciples who could turn the other cheek and go the second mile, who could leave their nets to become fishers of men, who could be tested by powers and principalities and would test well. Jesus sought those who would have no fear of the test, or at least if they had fear would not be paralyzed by it. He sought persons of character who would be able to face the test and those who would put the best face on it. And so in 1 Peter we read, "In this you rejoice, though now for a little while you may have to suffer various trials...." The author, with a gift for profound understatement, wrote a letter to Christians who were experiencing severe persecution by Rome. And so the Christians began the practice of gathering in obscure, out of the way places, to encourage one another to rejoice and to praise God and to worship God, even in the underground places of entombment — the catacombs —where they could honor those martyred in the faith and celebrate their life in the Lord.

Do you have the ability to test well and to rejoice? In your tests and in your trials, can you hear the voices of God's messengers who say, "Fear not, have no fear"? Will the genuineness of your faith, more precious than gold, redound (which means "echo") to praise and glory and honor at the revelation of Jesus Christ? Will the genuineness of your faith, the authenticity, the realness, the sincerity, the truth of your faith echo in praise and in glory and in honor because of how you are when you are tested — rejoicing? Will the genuineness of your faith echo because without having seen him you love him? Though you do not see him, do you believe in him and rejoice with unutterable joy? Did Christ call you because *you test well*? Rejoice so that the genuineness of your faith may echo ... in praise ... in glory ... in honor ... in this world and in the world to come.

---

1. Bryan Ethier, "Breaking the Sound Barrier," *American History*, September/ October 1997, pp. 24 -26

A Time To Be Born Anew

1 Peter 1:17-23

A man comes to Jesus by night, a ruler of the Jews; his name is Nicodemus. "Rabbi we know that you are come from God, for we have seen the signs that you do..." and if Nicodemus comes with a question he does not get it out before Jesus responds:

"Unless one is born anew, he cannot see the kingdom of God."

"How can a man be born when he is old? Can he enter a second time into his mother's womb and be born?" Nicodemus wonders aloud (John 3:1-4, author paraphrase).

And so the Gospel of John places the question on the table: What does it mean to be born anew? First Peter makes the striking assertion that through Christ we have confidence in God and that we have "been born anew, not of perishable seed but of imperishable, through the living and abiding word of God ..." (1 Peter 1:23).

So what does it mean to be born anew? We observe that folks in Christ's Church have widely divergent points of view on the question. Have you been born anew; are you a Christian, born again? Important questions for us to revisit, because sometimes persons who long for and try to claim new life in Christ look like the life is being squeezed out of them and wonder if new life has been stillborn. How much difference should it make if I am born anew, if I confess Christ as Lord, profess to be a follower of Jesus?

Conventional wisdom suggests that it does not have to make much of a difference. You will get along better in the world if you take your religion in moderation, like the tanning booth and Hagen Daaz ice cream. In fact, if one is born anew, one might be well advised to try not to act like it, for co-workers and friends could be put off by a newly born, newly saved person. You might not want to talk about being *saved* in polite company, because someone could become concerned that you would try to *save* him.

As an old lifeguard and teacher of lifeguards, I have to admit that these words create an odd ring in my ears. Before I was a lifeguard I was saved, and if I hadn't have been saved I would not be here preaching this sermon, and I would never have become a lifeguard or a teacher of lifesaving. I almost drowned as a kid and was saved, a story which is very interesting to me but one I will save for another day. The thing which is curious to me is that I have never met a person who was worried about being saved, if he or she *needed* to be saved.

Sometimes lifeguards save people before they are fully aware that they are in trouble. This usually happens with children. In shallow water a child, learning to swim and little by little gaining confidence, starts to bob. The child moves into deeper water still very much under control, but now gravity and inertia begin to take over. The bottom slopes away from the child's feet and the satis-fied, confident expression on the child's face turns to uncertainty with a hint of worry. The experienced lifeguard knows two or three more bobs into deeper and deeper water and the uncertainty of the child will turn into uncontrolled panic and utter terror. Now is the time to act. If the lifeguard moves quickly, the guard can often reach the child before the child comprehends the reality of the danger.

Parents and grandparents of young children know this scenario well. They frequently act to protect and/or save young children from danger, often when the children don't understand the poten-tial for trouble.

"The Church Is In The Saving Business"

It is hard to find common ground on this statement among Chris-tians. Some will only agree that the Church is in the saving busi-ness if we suggest that the Church is here to save the poor from hunger and poverty, and the oppressed from the ravages of oppres-sion and that this is how God saves. I could not agree more that this is a part of the Church's saving agenda, but this does not get us off the hook when we are inclined to say with Nicodemus: "How can a man be born when he is old? Can he enter a second time into his mother's womb and be born?"

To be born anew, to be a Christian, born again, to be saved is a foreign notion to some, because they view themselves as having been good most of their lives, they have never been a criminal or an addict, and life has never been desparately out of control so that God's agent of grace had to dive into the raging waters of sin and despair to save. And if in hearing this you think "that's me," we say our prayer of thankgiving that life for you has been good.

But it is also possible that some of us here are failing to give God the glory which is rightfully God's. "Can a man be born when he is old?" Nicodemus asks Christ. I want us for a few moments to think of "born anew" in a different frame. When was the last time you were borne?

When was the last time you were carried? I know this is a different kind of borne, it is spelled differently, but it will help us make our point.

When you were a baby, you were borne everywhere. When you were a child, maybe until you were ten or so, occasionally late at night you were borne to your bed and tucked in. When you had your accident, you were borne to the hospital. On your wedding day, you were borne to the church in fancy transportation. In your grief, you were borne by friends. In your education, you were borne by wonderful teachers. In your vocation, you are borne by all of the practitioners who went before you, by their invention, knowlege, and dedication. In your home, you are borne by tradition, common wisdom, commitment, and self control. And when you are old, one day your body will be borne by loved ones and friends to a final resting place and your spirit will be borne to God on the wings of love.

Will you be borne anew? Of course you will, again and again. But whether or not you sense it, whether or not you see it, whether or not you understand it, this will make all the difference for you as you seek to know the One who came to save, the One who bears you up not only on your last day but also on this day, in these days.

Who would you be if God had not borne you and borne everyone you love? Who would you be now, this moment, if God did not continually bear you? Who will you be, how can you be, if beginning this instant God does not bear you?

We remember the story which is often told of a dreamer who is walking with the Lord on a beach. Across the skies flash scenes from his life and mostly during his life journey there are two sets of footprints in the sand. Many times though he notices only one set of footprints, especially at the lowest and saddest times. And the dreamer asks the Lord about this; "I noticed that in the saddest and lowest times only one set of footprints appeared. I thought you promised to walk with me always. Why is it that you left me, especially when I needed you?"

"Dear child, in your times of trial, I did not leave. You see one set of footprints; this is where I carried you."

A wonderful and meaningful story, and it raises a question for us today. A question that gets close to the heart of the matter: "Can we imagine a time when in reality there is ever more than *one set of footprints* in the sand? When God Almighty did not carry us?"

Can we realize how much we have been saved? How much life and love is a gift? How the sustenance of this life is amazing grace?

Have you been born anew? If you have missed knowing how much you have been carried, then, probably not.

But if you have sensed how much you have been borne, how much you have been carried, how much you have been blessed, then ... The answer is self-evident.

Early in his ministry Jesus was teaching in a house near the Sea of Galilee and the power of the Lord was upon him to heal. Now there was a paralyzed man who was being brought to Jesus by his friends on a bed. They sought to have Jesus lay hands upon the paralyzed man, but the house where Christ was teaching was filled, overflowing with people standing on tiptoes at doorways and windows trying to see and hear. So finding no way in, the loving friends carried the paralyzed man to the roof and handed him down with his bed through the ceiling tiles into the midst of the crowd before Jesus. Christ saw the love and the faith of this man and his friends and tenderly said, "Man, your sins are forgiven you." Now the Pharisees who were nearby were shocked. "Who can forgive sins but God only?" they thought. And seeing their questions, Jesus answered them, "Which is easier, to say, 'Your sins are forgiven you,' or to say, 'Rise and walk'?" And then he said to the man, "I say to you, rise, take up your bed and go home." And the man who had been hopelessly paralyzed rose from his bed, took up that on which he had lain, and went home (Luke 5:17-25, author paraphrase).

Is there ever really more than one set of footprints in the sand? Is there ever a time when God does not carry us? Do we believe that anything we say or do has an enduring quality? Is any monument made with human hands fitting for the portals of eternity? Aren't the footprints we leave like the scratchings of a sparrow on the Rock of Gibraltar? The footprints in the sand and on the beach which endure are the footprints of God. The impression *we are* privileged to make is the impression of love left upon the heart of our loving Father, the etching of our faces and our lives left on the heart of our Parent who loves us and remembers us, cares for us, and watches over us. First Peter suggests, "Having purified your souls by your obedience to the truth for a sincere love of the brethren, love one another earnestly from the heart. You have been born anew, not of perishable seed but of imperishable, through the living and abiding word of God (1 Peter 1: 22-23).

We have the great and glorious chance to make our lasting, loving impression when we understand how God has borne us in every moment, and we open our hearts to God in love. God loves us and remembers us with fondness and tenderness when we love one another, when we carry each other as He has carried us even on the bed of our paralysis to the place of grace to be touched and healed and made whole. Do you understand how God has borne us, has carried us, has claimed us, has called and *saved us* from spending the gift of life pursuing things other than His love?

The Easter season is a time when we proclaim Christ's victory, when we name God victorious. May he also be victorious in every one of us as God bears us up not only in times of trial, not only in times of paralysis and pain, but also in times of carefree wandering, traveling, and reveling in the paths God allows us to choose until that day when earthly life and light grow dim and He bears us up to take us home.

A Time To See Through Suffering

1 Peter 2:19-25

"Oh, that had to hurt!" one brother said, looking down at the other sprawled on the backyard grass. Moments earlier the "quarterback" brother had thrown a pass to the "wide receiver" brother who had dived to make a spectacular catch, misjudging the location of a smallish tree, bruising a shoulder, elbow, and knee before crashing onto the turf, moaning. It is true; in our lives there is pain. It is true; there is suffering.

"He used to be such a fine father to the girls," she said. "I just don't know what got into him." Years later it is still baffling to the single mom who had done her best to get over the sudden departure of her husband. "He said his life just wasn't fulfilling. It sure has made things more complicated around here." The mom has since gone back to work and is considering picking up a second job. "I'm just not sure. We could use the money, but that time is my time with the girls."

"I feel like I've done everything they ask. And yet, my department has been down-sized by half. I know I could be next. It's frustrating to know that it doesn't matter whether you're doing a good job or not. They're just going a different direction with the company. And at my age — I'm too young to retire, but I can't think it's going to be easy finding another company which wants me."

"Mom was doing just great, most of the time. It was really impressive that at her age she could still live alone, drive, and be as busy as she was. Then we got the call saying she'd fallen and it was her hip. Well, I was afraid it would come to this. I think the surgery took something out of her. It's like she's just lost her will to keep going."

"Charles was always such a good boy. His grades were never what his sister's were, but he seemed to be pretty well-rounded. When he got to high school though, it just seems like he got involved with the wrong crowd. Of course that was the same time I was traveling more with work. I guess I didn't have as much time to spend with him. When I got home last week and Mary said she found something that looked like marijuana in his room, I just lost it. He said it wasn't his, he was just keeping it for a friend . . ."

"Her times have been good all year. She's always been the fastest or second fastest girl in her age group in the state, and it was clear that if she had a decent senior season, there was a good chance she would be offered a scholarship to a really great school. But they said that the knee is hurt pretty badly. It looks like a ligament, and who knows what else. Well, one thing we know, she won't be running anytime soon."

It is true that in our lives there is pain; there is suffering. And while to escape our pain, suffering, and anxiety we may watch a television drama or film which finds neat resolution in an hour or two, our suffering and our pain hardly ever resolves so neatly or quickly and nearly always marks us.

As a young man I delivered the early morning paper in my neighborhood. I found it an exhilarating experience, especially in the winter when the earth was blanketed with snow. The silence created by the quieting snow cover and the brightness of night under a full moon created a spiritual quality as I wandered from house to house, gently pitching the papers onto porches. Delivering the news wasn't always so pristine however.

One spring morning with the sun nearly up over the horizon, I was riding my bicycle and had almost completed my route. My front wheel caught a rut and pitched me sideways and forward, forcing me to land awkwardly on my hand. Picking myself off the pavement, I saw the end of my thumb hanging by a thread of skin. There was nothing to do but get back on my bicycle and ride home, where I awakened my sleeping parents. At a glance, assessing my problem, Mom said to Dad, "We need to go to the emergency room;

he's torn off the end of his thumb." All was a flurry for partly wakened parents, pulling clothes on, concerned for my condition, until Dad asked in groggy confusion, "Well, how can he talk, if he bit off the end of his tongue?!" To this day, one of my thumbs is a little shorter and a little blunter than the other. When pain and suffering come, it marks us, changes us. In First Peter suffering under deserved punishment is contrasted with suffering which is unjust and undeserved. The clarity of this distinction is not necessarily as easily identified as would be implied in the epistle.

Cross Or Crop

In our world, there are striking examples of those who suffer unjustly for righteousness. Two good examples are Nelson Mandella's imprisonment, and the attempted assassination of Pope John Paul II and his moving audience with his assassin and subsequent forgiveness of him. Likewise suffering "just punishment" as imprisonment or fines, though part of our culture, is hardly the limit of the suffering we incur due to our own actions. How many surgeries have been performed in a large measure because of the dietary habits of patients? How many other lifestyle choices have health implications which eventually result in suffering? We have concerns about how we have treated our environment and what long-term effect these actions may have on our quality of life on this planet. So sometimes suffering comes as a result of our own actions and it is worth asking: Is this a *cross* to bear or a *crop* resulting from careless planting? But such a distinction is not the focus of our text in any case.

While certain kinds of suffering can be endured as a witness to the faith and for the inspiration for all, our *response* to suffering often has an element of spirituality in it. When a mother gives birth, as Lamaze reminds us, if she has a point of focus, the mother can see past the pain; she can see through the suffering. When the pain is great, the laboring mother is trained to focus on a photograph of her family or an item of particular meaning or comfort. We can learn from this in our times of suffering. Focus beyond the suffering to that which is of fundamental importance to us and our endurance of suffering will be filled with grace and gracefulness. Those who suffer most focus on their suffering and cultivate an anger toward it. But those who peacefully persevere, carrying discomfort with a calm, courageous capacity find freedom from the prison of pain and glory in a God-desiring and God-focused attention.

Getting Past The Pain

What kind of witness is it when Christian discipleship costs little or nothing? Things which are worth pursuing require something of us. Do you eat your peas with a knife? Probably not, but even if you don't, does it say much about your character? How hard is it to play music at a reasonable level on your stereo? But if you are a good stereo citizen, what does it really say about your character? How hard is it to drive a mile in six minutes? How about run a mile in six minutes? How hard is it to play a disc on your Walkman? How hard is it to play Beethoven on the piano? Or how hard is it to replace the glass in a storm door? But how much more difficult is it to replace the stained glass rose window of the Cathedral of Notre Dame? Learning to persevere through the pain, to see through the suffering with God-desiring, God-focused attention is similar to the mental and spiritual maturity required for significant athletic or artistic achievement. In this life we are all — remembering the words of Isaiah — men and women of sorrow, and we are acquainted with grief. Most of us are stricken, smitten, afflicted, and more than a few times. And as we see through the suffering, we are given the gift of sensitivity to the suffering of others. When we are afflicted, we better understand the afflictions of others. When we are stricken, we better understand others who are stricken. When we are in grief, or when we have had grief, we better understand those who are grieving. So in our times of weakness and brokenness, we are able to understand the weakness and brokenness of others, even the brokenness of Jesus, and to follow his example. On the cross, Christ also understood the suffering, pain, and affliction of others. "Father, forgive them, for they know not what they do." "When Jesus saw his mother and the disciple whom he loved standing near, he said to his mother, 'Woman, behold your son!' Then he said to the disciple, 'Behold, your mother!'

And from that hour the disciple took her to his home" (John 19:26, 27). Jesus was concerned about the condition and care of his mother. He saw through his suffering to the pain of his mother and to the affliction of us all.

And so may it be for you. That you might see through the suffering, becoming more sensitive to the suffering of others even to the suffering of Christ, even to the suffering of God. And then may you find comfort. Hear these words from the beginning of Second Corinthians:

> *Blessed be the God and Father of our Lord Jesus Christ, the Father of mercies and God of all comfort, who comforts us in all our affliction, so that we may be able to comfort those who are in any affliction, with the comfort with which we ourselves are comforted by God. For as we share abundantly in Christ's sufferings, so through Christ we share abundantly in comfort, too.*
>
> — 2 Corinthians 1:3-5

And so may we be approved by God in our suffering even as we see through it with a God-desiring, God-focused attention to the suffering of others, even as we are marked by it and changed by it. And when we are afflicted, may we be drawn closer to God and find comfort in His love.

A Time To Build Another Story On A Stone House

1 Peter 2:2-10

There was much excitement in the summer of '64 at Tell Makor in Israel. Digging and sifting, digging and sifting, as two exploratory trenches were sunk into the earth where, millennium upon millennium, people ever more civilized and refined had lived. A tell is a place where, because of strategic advantage and fresh water, villages and cities have been created and destroyed over a long period of time. One city built on the ashes of another, allowing a careful archeologist to study in one location the many stages of civilization. James Michener in his novel *The Source* tells the story of Tell Makor. Funding the expedition is a wealthy Chicagoan whose imagination has been titillated by the possibility of finding the remains of a crusader's castle. The imagination of the archeologists at the site runs much deeper. In 1964 digging at such a site was done by hand: hot, hard, slow, careful work. After many days at Tell Makor they came upon a stone inscribed with the year 1105 A.D. Word went out, "It looks as if we've hit the castle!" And so careful work began in the recovery of crusader era artifacts.

But in the second exploratory trench there were no finds of the magnitude of a castle, so work continued, layer by layer finding artifacts as each layer of habitation was penetrated: a stone from a place of worship which showed signs that in different times Muslim, Christian, and Jewish congregations had occupied its walls; a Roman coin dated 70 A.D.; a portion of Greek statuary, 165 B.C.; a Babylonian spear point and soldier's helmet, 600 B.C.; a horned Hebrew altar dated 1000 B.C.; a clay fertility goddess, 2000 B.C.; a flint sickle, 10,000 B.C. Twelve thousand years ago, "in some mysterious way he [the owner of the sickle] had made grain grow where he wanted it, and with the sickle to aid him, had been able to settle down and start a village that had become in time the site of a Roman city, of a fine Byzantine church and a towering crusader's castle."[1] Soon after the finding of the sickle, the archeologists and their team hit bedrock, and the long hard exploratory digging stopped.

In First Peter we read, "Come to him, to that living stone, rejected by men but in God's sight chosen and precious; and like living stones be yourselves built into a spiritual house ..." (1 Peter 2:4-5). At Tell Makor the story of human civilization is told by stones and artifacts piled one layer upon another, and James Michener weaves together the stories of the people of the many layers to form a long, wonderful novel. And likewise our sacred story in many ways is a story of stones marking our journey with God — like ancient mile markers placed along the Roman highway, through wilderness roads to a land of promise, into exile, and on the road of return from exile. Our sacred history is a journey of stories and stones of God's people looking expectantly to the distance for the next story and the next stone.

In Genesis we learn the story of Jacob, son of Isaac, traveling between Beer-sheba and Haran, who in a certain place stayed for the night. He laid down his head on one of the stones from the place and began to dream. In his dream he saw a ladder set up between heaven and earth. And he saw the angels of God ascending and descending on it. "And behold, the Lord stood above it and said, 'I am the Lord, the God of Abraham your father and the God of Isaac; the land on which you lie I will give to you and to your descendants. And your descendants shall be like the dust of the earth, and you shall spread abroad to the west and to the east and to the north and to the south and by you and your descendants shall all the families of the earth bless themselves. Behold, I am with you and will keep you wherever you go ...' " And Jacob awoke from sleep and knew that the Lord was in that place. In the morning he took the stone which had been under his head and set it on a pillar and poured oil on it. He called that place Bethel, which means house of God (Genesis 28:10-18, author paraphrase).

86

Jacob marked that place with a stone and called it God's house. Some distance on, down the highway of history, we see another stone marker. Moses and Aaron stand together with the elders of Israel. They stand near a great stone, the stone of Sinai the Mountain. Moses receives the instruction from the Lord to come up on the mountain and the promise that Moses will receive tables of stone — the law and the commandment. So Moses entered the cloud which is the presence of the Lord and stayed on the stone of Sinai forty days and forty nights. He returned from the Lord with tables of stone for the instruction and guidance of the people of God, and we learn from them even to this day.

And, at a distance on the highway of history, we find more stones, five smooth stones held in the hand of a boy standing before a great and threatening giant of a man. The giant scoffs at the lad who whirls a stone in a leather sling and unleashes its power. With the crashing of armor on the stones of the ground, the giant falls because of the power of a stone in the hand of a fearless boy who was faithful to God.

And on the highway of history in the distance there is Jesus on the temple, tempted. "If you are the Son of God, throw yourself down for it is written, 'He will give his angels charge of you,' and 'on their hands they will bear you up, lest you strike your foot against a stone' " (Matthew 4:6). Jesus spoke to us of stones, "Let him who is without sin among you be the first to throw a stone ..." (John 8:7).

> *And he said, "Whoever humbles himself like this child, he is the greatest in the kingdom of heaven. Whoever receives one such child in my name receives me; but whoever causes one of these little ones who believe in me to sin, it would be better for him to have a great millstone fastened round his neck and to be drowned in the depths of the sea."* — Matthew 18:4-6

And on the highway of history in the distance there is a stone; it is in the midst of a garden and the earth is shaking — a great earthquake. "For an angel of the Lord descended from heaven and came and rolled back the stone, and sat upon it." The guards trembled and were paralyzed with fear becoming like dead men (Matthew 28:2-4).

We receive the instruction in First Peter "Like living stones be yourselves built into a spiritual house ... For it stands in scripture: 'Behold, I am laying in Zion a stone, a corner stone chosen and precious ... the very stone which the builders rejected has become the head of the corner ...' " (1 Peter 2:5-7). Be yourselves built into a spiritual house like living stones — a house made of stones with Christ as its cornerstone. Build on Christ, on the good foundation as stones being constructed into a spiritual house.

One of the great accomplishments in the building of the Golden Gate Bridge in the 1930s was that the second 746 foot tower, roughly the size of a 65-story skyscraper was *placed on bedrock* out in the entrance of San Francisco Bay — *bedrock* that was 65 feet below the surface of the water. In the 1930s it was an amazing achievement to build on bedrock six-and-a-half stories deep under water. But if we are to build anywhere, it is important to be on a good foundation. Be as living stones constructed into a spiritual house built on the cornerstone of Christ, the good foundation. Our highway of history is marked by stories and stones, and collected, they are constructed together into a spiritual house and we have a cornerstone which is Christ, a firm foundation for our building. But this house which is constructed of stones needs a new level, a new story. It is our story as we are the living stones to be constructed and Christ is the head of the corner. In First Peter we read, "Like new born babes long for the pure spiritual milk, that by it you may grow up to salvation; for you have tasted the kindness of the Lord." Now it is time for our level in the tell of history. It is time for our story of the spiritual house. God is building it, writing it, even in these days. But let us not allow ourselves to be left out of this construction. Let us not be cast aside or be found unacceptable in the building of this story for this is our time, and this is our opportunity to be crafted in the hands of the Master Builder as living stones into a house solid and sure and true, built on the cornerstone which is Christ who is our good foundation. Once you were no people, but now you are God's people; once you had not received mercy, but now you have received mercy; once you had no story, now you are part of God's story. So be built into a stone house and may your story, may our story, be as good, as strong, and as faithful as those which have gone before.

---

1. James A. Michener, *The Source* (New York: Random House, 1965), p. 82.

A Time To Come Along, Bravely

1 Peter 3:13-22

The waiting room is adequate but nothing fancy; magazines dog-eared and out of date, a few toys for the children help with the cramped, crowded feeling. Some parents have brought along toys and books from home. One poor dad with the fussiest child is doing the best he can with his car keys to entertain his little girl; in a couple of minutes she has lost interest.

Mary has brought her two daughters. She believes one of them has an ear infection, but these days where one goes, they all go. It wasn't easy getting out of the house for an early appointment; Mary remembered the crackers and juice boxes, but forgot the toys. There is a puzzle the girls might like, but another child is using it. Only the healthy one feels like playing anyway. During the short drive to the doctor's office the girls were remembering when they last got shots. By the time they arrived Amy, the sick one, wouldn't get out of the car. Finally Mommy promises to ask the doctor not to give her a shot. Mary is now wearily reading to Amy and the healthy daughter has gotten ahold of the puzzle. Near the puzzle table, a door swings open, held wide by a friendly-looking nurse in a brightly colored uniform, "Amy?" She looks right at Mary and Amy. Amy buries her head in Mary's shoulder and finally stands up. Mary gathers her things and takes Amy's hand, "Come along, Amy, be brave. You'll be just fine." And with that, the tentative trio moves toward the examining rooms.

"Come along, be brave," Jesus said to Peter and Andrew, James and John, Matthew and Philip and the others. "Come along, be brave," Jesus says to us, or was it ..."Follow me"?

91

"Now who is there to harm you if you are zealous for what is right? But even if you do suffer for righteousness' sake you will be blessed" (1 Peter 3:13-14).

Do you remember Noah? How God called him to build an ark? How the flood waters came, and how he and his wife and his sons and their wives boarded the ark with all of the animals? Because Noah had been faithful, God said to him, "Come along, be brave. You'll be fine."

"Come along, be brave," is easy to say, but sadly in our world we know we won't necessarily be just fine.

An executive quits his job on principle. He feels better about himself because he has finally stood up to his boss's dishonesty. Six months later, he is still out of work. He has always advised others: don't leave a job before you have another one lined up, but this time it seemed different. However, with two young children at home, and a third on the way, he's not so sure he did the right thing.

"Now who is there to harm you if you are zealous for what is right?" we read in First Peter, a letter written to the Christians under the very severe persecution of Rome. These Christians had to be excited and pleased about receiving this letter, but I wonder if they were equally excited when they considered its content. "But even if you do suffer for righteousness sake, you will be blessed. Have no fear ..." (1 Peter 3:13-14).

The drama is nearing its conclusion. The convent is being searched by the Nazis and the nuns are readying the von Trapp family for their escape in a car belonging to the caretaker. News comes that the borders have been closed, to which Captain von Trapp responds, "Well, then we'll drive up into the mountains and cross the border on foot!"[1] The scene from the movie/musical, though not historically accurate since the real von Trapp family made its escape by rail, is a wonderful image for us today: the von Trapps, practically of every age from the parents to the young children, climbing every mountain under a crystal blue sky to safety and freedom. "Come along, be brave. You'll be fine." And they did and they were just fine.

But six million Jews exterminated in Nazi death camps remind us, when we are called to "Come along, bravely," that is, "Come along and have no fear," it is best also to come along, *carefully*.

We know the Old Testament story of Joseph, how his brothers hated him, and likely for good reason. He was the apple of his father's eye and gave definition to the word "spoiled." So his brothers devised a plan. They were out in the wilderness watching their father's flocks and saw from a distance Joseph coming to check on them. They wanted to capture Joseph, kill him, and throw him into a pit and let wild animals devour him. So much for brotherly love! But one brother prevailed upon his other brothers to throw Joseph into the pit without killing him. Reuben was secretly hoping to return to rescue Joseph. Reuben said to them, "Shed no blood; cast him into this pit here in the wilderness, but lay no hand upon him..." (Genesis 37:22). So this they did, casting Joseph into a pit. And as they sat down to eat, a caravan of Ish'maelites drew near. Now they pulled Joseph up out of the pit and the brothers sold him to the Mid'ianite traders for twenty shekels of silver, sending Joseph with the caravan to Egypt.

Joseph was sent out by his father to check on his brothers who were tending his father's flocks, "Go along Joseph, be brave, *be careful!*" And Joseph wound up in Egypt.

You have heard of Oscar Schindler and Raoul Wallenberg, but have you heard of Tina Strobos, Mirjam Pinkof, or Barbara Makuch?[2]

In the Netherlands, the medical student, Tina Strobos, went bravely to the aid of numerous Jewish people during the Nazi occupation of her country. Tina, with her mother and grandmother, gave shelter to many, sometimes for nearly a year. Tina was active in the Dutch underground and helped Jews with food and false identity papers, and with finding places of refuge with other Dutch families. Once when four of her Jewish friends were found and arrested, Tina's calm persuasion convinced a high ranking S.S. officer to set three of them free. "Go along, Tina, be brave, be careful."

Mirjam Pinkhof was instrumental in creating a group that helped hundreds of Jewish teenagers and children survive the Holocaust.

93

Mirjam, who was Jewish herself and in constant danger, chose to ignore the safe route and instead remained in Holland to help children who had been sent there from Germany by parents hoping that at least their children might live. Mirjam worked tirelessly to find hiding places for these children in Holland, and many eventually were smuggled to France, which was safer. Some even made it, before the war ended, to Spain and Palestine. "Go along, Mirjam, be brave, *be careful.*"

Barbara Makuch was a teacher in a boy's boarding school where she helped one Jewish boy assume the identity of a Christian Polish student. On another occasion she helped a Jewish woman physician find refuge as the school cook. Barbara later assumed, from a desperate mother, care of a seven-year-old Jewish girl. Because of her fear of discovery, Barbara and the girl made the dangerous trip to a larger town, where the girl was safely placed in a convent school. Barbara was finally caught while acting as a courier for the underground and imprisoned in a German concentration camp. During the years in prison, Barbara Makuch faced many harsh tests. Amazingly she survived and remarkably helped save the lives of several fellow inmates. "Go along, Barbara, be brave, *be careful.*"

And so the writer of First Peter has more than a few reasons to fear, but writes, "Have no fear...." Later in their lives those brothers of Joseph who had sold him into bondage had reason to fear. There was a great famine in the land and so they traveled to Egypt in search of food. Through a variety of circumstances Joseph while living in Egypt had found favor with Pharaoh and had attained a prominent place in the Egyptian court. It is a scene filled with irony as the brothers come asking Joseph, whom they do not recognize, for food. Will Joseph be consumed by anger and delight in vengefulness?

Joseph played a little trick on his brothers, but then revealed his identity to them.

> *So Joseph said to his brothers, "Come near to me, I pray you." And they came near. And he said, "I am your brother, Joseph, whom you sold into Egypt. And now do not be*

distressed, or angry with yourselves, because you sold me here; for God sent me before you to preserve life...."
— Genesis 45:4-9

He explained to his brothers his position and role in the Egyptian Court and discussed with them the famine in their homeland. And then he sent them home to bring to Egypt their father and his household. Say to my father, "This is a message from Joseph: Come along, Father, be brave, be careful, *be welcome.*"

And so the message echoes through the centuries until even it falls upon our ears. "Now who is there to harm you if you are zealous for what is right? But even if you do suffer for righteousness' sake, you will be blessed" (1 Peter 3:13-14). "Come along, bravely." How would we feel if Christ came to us with those words today, even now? "Come along, bravely." Is there a readiness in you and in me to hear him beckon us by name to come along? Would we be ready to leave behind what we know of this life and be confident in his calling? And would we be brave?

If our answer is yes, then we are ready also to hear his calling to *come along* in this life. We are prepared to be among those who have already left behind everything to follow him. And we are brave enough to go where he will send us, to city council to speak his mind, to teach the middle school Sunday school class, to the soup kitchen where each week we kick in a little extra to make the broth thicker and more tasty, or to the home of someone on our street who can't get out anymore and just wants to talk.

I expect we are brave enough to do these things and to follow him when he calls.

So go, be careful, and be brave.

---

1. *The Sound of Music*, copyright 1965: Argyle Enterprises and Twentieth Century Fox Film Corporation.

2. Ellen Land-Weber, *To Save a Life: Stories of Jewish Rescue*, copyright 1996. http://sorrel.humbolt.edu/~rescuers/book/contents.html
The stories of Tina Strobos, Mirjam Pinkhof, Barbara Makuch are beautifully told at this web address.

A Time To Hear Hope Calling

Ephesians 1:15-23

Huckle the Cat and his school teacher Miss Honey the Bear, Bananas Gorilla, Captain Salty, Pig Will and Pig Won't, Sergeant Murphy the Police Dog, and my favorite, Lowly the Worm; if you know these names then you are familiar with the work of Richard Scarry, author and illustrator of children's books, who passed away in '94 at age 75. Scarry wrote over 250 books, which in thirty languages have sold over 100 million copies. He said, "The greatest compliment I can receive is to be told that some of my books are held together with more Scotch tape than there is paper in the original book. They've been used so much, they've been torn to pieces."[1]

In the many Richard Scarry books, the character most intriguing to me is Mr. Fix It the Fox. Mr. Fix It is the one in Busytown who fixes things and doesn't always get it right. And it is because today is the remembrance of Our Lord's Ascension that I mention Mr. Fix It. For in some ways Christ's disciples wanted him to be Mr. Fix It for them and for their community. There had been a great longing for a Messiah who would restore Israel, who would ascend to the throne of David and would reestablish the good fortune of the Hebrew people — God's chosen ones. So, when Jesus came and some began to proclaim him Messiah, there were certain expectations attached, that he might be God's Mr. Fix It finally come ... thus, his enthusiastic entrance into Jerusalem with palm branches waving.

But the view of this Messiah on the day of his ascension is quite different. The Book of Acts gives us the most vivid description of Christ's ascension. The Risen Christ appeared to the disciples over a stretch of forty days, encouraging and instructing those who would carry on his work. Then preparing to return to his Father, he told the disciples to wait in Jerusalem until they were empowered by the Holy Spirit.

And the disciples asked him:

> *Lord, will you at this time restore the kingdom to Israel?*
> *He said to them, "It is not for you to know times or*
> *seasons which the Father has fixed by his own authority.*
> *But you shall receive power when the Holy Spirit has come*
> *upon you; and you shall be my witnesses in Jerusalem*
> *and in all Judea and Samar' ia and to the end of the earth."*
> — Acts 1:6-8

And after Christ had said this, he was lifted up "and a cloud took him out of their sight" (v. 9) and they all stood there gazing into heaven, but two in white robes standing near called to them, "Men of Galilee, why do you stand looking into heaven? This Jesus, who was taken up from you into heaven, will come in the same way as you saw him go into heaven" (v. 11).

Then they returned to Jerusalem from Mount Olivet to *pray* and to *wait* for the coming of the Spirit. And the Spirit did come soon enough, with tongues as of fire and with rushing winds, and though for a time many expected the immediate return of Christ as an apocalyptic conclusion to history, the "pray and wait" instruction until the coming of the Spirit, became *"pray, wait, and work"* as the disciples picked up the ministry of Christ.

In Ephesians, Paul prays: "that the God of our Lord Jesus Christ ... may give you a spirit of wisdom and of revelation in the knowledge of him, having the eyes of your hearts enlightened, that you may know *what is the hope to which he has called you ...*" (Ephesians 1:17-18).

Christ went to heaven and his followers went to pray, wait, and work. Some wanted to pray and wait for the coming of the Lord, with no work. And this has always been true in the church. Some

98

are inclined to pray and wait, wait and pray, being drawn ever closer to God in mystic sweet communion. Some followers of Jesus are tempted to scoff at such an approach with its inner focus and lack of tangible fruitfulness, but if one reads the Christian mystics one is quick to realize that the mystical journey is often not an entirely sweet one and that there is more *work* involved than might be seen at a glance.

Many, however, picked up the *active* ministry of Jesus, healing the sick, caring for the lost, proclaiming that the Kingdom of God is at hand. This is true, of course, even in our time: followers of Jesus healing the sick, caring for the lost, preaching peace, proclaiming the Kingdom of God is at hand. These days most do not expect that Christ's return is scheduled in a few weeks or months or even at the turn of the millennium. Most expect to live out their days in his service, one day being prayed into heaven in a place such as this and remembered as faithful followers of the risen Christ.

So we are "Christians in between," awaiting the fulfillment of what God started by sending Jesus, doing the best we can to carry out his ministry, sometimes wondering if we are making progress, sometimes fairly sure we are losing ground, struggling sometimes to hold onto the hope Paul writes about and wishing a "Mr. Fix It" God would show up from time to time to take care of the things which are clearly broken.

Of course, occasionally almost all of us think of God as Mr. Fix It. We pray for God to fix our illnesses, our relationships, our indecision, and our selfishness, and to remove or lighten the burdens of others. And it is important for us to pray in this way because we know God welcomes the thoughts and desires of our hearts when earnestly brought to God in prayer. God is fully capable to sift out the trivialities and longs to be united to us in this way. But sometimes we Christians would be helped if we adjusted our expectations of the result of prayer. Sometimes when we pray, it sounds as though we believe the only successful prayers result in miracles of biblical proportion.

When Jesus raised Ja'irus' daughter from the dead, or Lazarus, there is no suggestion that from that moment on the two (or others for that matter whom Jesus blessed in special ways) went on to

99

lives free from life's major challenges. One day they all concluded their earthly lives, as will we. The delaying of death for Lazarus and Ja'irus' daughter is a sign of who Jesus is in our midst. And we need to thank God richly, even as did the families of Lazarus and Ja'irus, whenever we receive a sign of the profound ever-presence of God's love and God's power. We should not, however, expect God to prove God's love by being for us "Mr. Fix It." *God's love has already been proven!*

But it is true that there are more than a few things which need to be fixed, and we are proud and pleased to be a part of a community of faith which has set out to do some of the fixing. Dear friends, it is easy to be overcome with a feeling of haste, with a sense of urgency, and then on seeing the size of the task, to become discouraged. I think it is a thorn of the flesh or the spirit for every serious Christian. We all sometimes fight a feeling of futility. Where is the Power of Almighty God when we really need it, where is "Mr. Fix It," anyway?! What do you mean we are the ones through whom the Kingdom will come and, for the time being, it is through *us* that the *fixing* will happen? Can you hear Hope calling?

Can You Hear Hope Calling?

Paul prays for us in his letter to the Ephesians: "that the God of our Lord Jesus Christ ... may give you a spirit of wisdom and of revelation in the knowledge of him, having the eyes of your hearts enlightened, that you may know what is the hope to which he has called you ..." (Ephesians 1:17-18).

Jesus was lifted up, as we have proclaimed remembering Our Lord's Ascension, and we will be lifted up with him. We have been told that in the same way we saw him go, he will come. "A cloud took him out of their sight" (v. 9) and a cloud will bring him.

When life is clouded and unsure,
for you he will come.
When the path is fogged and frightening not only for
your self,
but for those you love,
he will come.

100

When the clouds provide gentle spring rain bringing joy
as the flowers of the earth again come forth,
he will come.
When the clouds are of storm and conflict,
for you he will come.
And when clouds seem to cover the whole earth,
he will come,
as he said he would.

Do You Hear Hope Calling?

Jesus Christ planted a church in Coventry, England, in 1043, first a Benedictine monastery, then the Cathedral of St. Michael, an inspiring Gothic structure. The service of St. Michael's was abruptly and forever changed when in 1940 the cathedral took a direct hit during a nighttime bombing raid. As fire brigades bravely tried to control the many fires in the huge structure, one portion of the fire burned especially bright. It was the pipe organ which had played God's music in thousands of services going back to the days when Handel had played the instrument. In the morning, when the smoke clouds lifted, only the main spire, a portion of the sanctuary cross, and a few sections of the exterior walls and arches remained. Coventry was stunned, as much by the loss of its cathedral as by the bombs themselves.

Within days of its destruction, the decision was made to rebuild the cathedral and to make the church a symbol of hope. But how could this be done? It was still 1940 and England was taking a pounding. Then out of the rubble a priest of the church picked up some nails and made them into a cross. The rebuilding of the church could not begin right away, it would have to wait until after the war. So in the clearing of the rubble, nails were collected, saved, and sent at war's end to churches in Germany and elsewhere, telling the story of the demolished church. In a little while, German students had organized themselves to come and assist in the reconstruction, which was carried on successfully to its completion in large measure because of the German students. A group was organized named the Community of the Cross of Nails and initially helped with the reconstruction of many churches across war-ravaged Europe, including Dresden, Germany.

101

The Community of the Cross of Nails is now an international organization for the promotion of reconciliation bringing together people from such places as Bosnia, Northern Ireland, the Middle East, and South Africa who seek solutions to conflict in our world.

When the old cathedral was rebuilt it was replaced with a modern structure, but the original spire, some surviving arches, and the damaged cross were kept in place in a large pedestrian mall adjacent to the new church. From the inside of the new cathedral through windows etched with angels, worshipers can see the old spire still standing and the arches, a reminder of what was and what happened ... They wanted to rebuild their church and they made it a symbol of hope. Can you hear hope calling?

Paul prays: "that the God of our Lord Jesus Christ ... may give you a spirit of wisdom and of revelation in the knowledge of him, having the eyes of your hearts enlightened, that you may know what is the hope to which he has called you ..." (Ephesians 1:17-18).

When Jesus left us, a cloud took him out of our sight. And when in our lives, clouds descend, even when they seem to cover the whole earth, *for you he will come as he promised.*

---

1. Laurie Lanzen Harris, *Biography for Beginners* (Detroit: Omnigraphics Inc., Spring 1995, Issue 1), p. 75.

A Time to Answer:
Where Do You Live?

1 Peter 4:12-14; 5:6-11

Where do you live? It's a question we ask sometimes. Where's your home? Where are you from? Where's home? is a good question. Sometimes, though folks live one place, if you ask them where is home, they will say someplace else, because home is where their parents live. Home is where they spent most of their life journey. Where do you live? Where's home?

346 Pattie Drive was home for us when I was young — a street of ranch-style houses with shingles on the side. A few doors down, there was a family with a color television, and when our relations were good they'd invite us to come over and see *The Wonderful World of Color.* It was a place where a man delivered milk and juice to our door and where sometimes the Fuller Brush man stopped. Where's your home? 346 Pattie Drive is near Cleveland, near Baldwin-Wallace College. Did *you* grow up on a farm? in a different state? in a different country?

In many towns across our land an interesting phenomenon takes place: the North/South High School basketball game. Change the names of the schools and maybe even the sport, and the time-honored tradition of the sports rivalry is played out over and over. Where do you live? Where is your home? Where do your children go to school? Where's your loyalty? Oh, how important it is to know where your children go to school: to North or to South High School, until maybe you are a thousand miles from home and someone says to you, "Where's your home; where are you from?"

"Ohio? I'm from Ohio, too! What a great place."

103

We have friends from that state up north (Michigan). I must say that my Ohio State Buckeye fan father was probably one who strained to be friends with folks from that state, but I have seen the error of his ways. But even for the most ardent like my dad, if you put him halfway around the world stationed with U.S. armed forces, he'd say: "You from Michigan? Well, I'm from the Midwest, too!" Where are you from? Where is your home?

Jesus has something to say to us about this as well. "Abide in me and I in you, as the branch cannot bear fruit by itself unless it abides in the vine. Neither can you unless you abide in me." Where is your home? He is your home. "Abide in me."

When I was a child I was so proud to have learned my address: 346 Pattie Drive. I located myself in that community, which I thought was my entire world.

We are a campus church. When students come to campus we ask, "Where is your home?"

For a while they tell us about their hometown, but after they have been on campus for a few quarters, they respond: "I live in the Hanby dorm." Where is your home?

"Well, I grew up on a farm. Oh, what I'd give to be back there these days — to see the spring, to see the sun shine across the fields at dawn."

In a recent adventure film, a fellow was thrown by dastardly villains out of an airplane. He falls, and with increasing panic, tries to get his parachute open, with little success. Finally nearing the ground, the chute pops open. The fellow, at a speed too fast for human health, lands crashing on top of a junked car. A brother and sister playing nearby are startled and look up. From on top of the car the parachuter sees the children. "Where am I?" he asks. With widening eyes the little girl responds, "Earth — welcome!"

Where is your home?

In today's text, Peter is concerned with where you live, how you live, and the conditions under which you live. Peter is writing to first century Christians and to us. In the first century, Christians were undergoing great hardship; Rome had been burned and the Emperor Nero was severely persecuting the Christians whom he suspected of the arson.

Peter writes: "Beloved, do not be surprised at the fiery ordeal which comes upon you to prove you, as though something strange were happening to you. But rejoice in so far as you share Christ's sufferings, that you may also rejoice and be glad when his glory is revealed" (1 Peter 4:12-13). His words encourage these Christians who are in the midst of a terrible situation, and assure them that their suffering has meaning. Suffering gives them even greater grounding as followers of Christ and connects them even more intimately with the glory of God.

We often do not have ultimate control over very significant parts of our lives: our health, our relationships, our employment, the length of our lives. Peter instructs us to live in our circumstances with hope and confidence, and when suffering comes to know that suffering connects us even more fully to God.

Jesus sent out seventy disciples, two by two, and he said to them, "Whatsoever house you enter into, there abide, there live" (see Luke 10:1-7). Jesus was traveling through Jericho with a great throng around him. A certain man not large of stature wanted to see Jesus. He perched in a sycamore tree to improve his view. Jesus seeing him in the tree said, "Zacchaeus come down from there." He said, "Zacchaeus come down from there, *for today I must abide in your house*" (see Luke 19:2-5). Abide in me and I in thee which is to say, live in the place where life brings you, and be assured that in each circumstance, in joy and in sorrow, in happiness and in suffering, I abide with thee.

After the resurrection, there were two travelers on the road talking about the things which had occurred in Jerusalem — about how Jesus had been crucified, had been laid in a tomb, and had been raised on the third day. A stranger came upon these travelers and walked with them. They explained to him the recent events at Jerusalem. The stranger in turn explained to the two travelers how this was the fulfillment of the Word and opened for them the scriptures. As they drew near to the village of Emmaus, the destination of the two, the stranger appeared to be going on farther. They said to him, "Come, abide with us, for it is toward evening and the day is far spent." So the stranger went to stay with them. And as they shared a meal, the stranger made himself known to them, revealing himself to be Jesus, in the breaking of the bread (Luke 24:13-31).

Abide with me and I with thee. Where is your home? Your home is in him. Your home, in him. In the fourteenth chapter of John, Jesus tells his disciples: "Let not your hearts be troubled; believe in God, believe also in me. In my father's house are many abiding places. If it were not so would I have told you that I go to prepare an abiding place for you? And when I go and prepare an abiding place for you, I will come again and will receive you unto myself, that where I abide, you may abide also" (see John 14:1-3).

Where is your home? Where is your heart's true home?

Today we address two key concerns. First: Where's your home? Where will you abide? The second: *The father is the vine dresser and there is some pruning that happens and suffering which occurs.*

Do you know certain plants prune themselves? If a branch is useless, it dies off and falls to the ground. But there are other plants that need to be pruned, and this pruning is never pleasant. They need a vine dresser or a gardener to do the pruning. And pruning is more than shaping.

When I was a little fellow, my dad used to be my barber. There was always relative chaos in our family when my dad would try to cut our hair (there were three boys). My mother would supervise and have too many opinions. She would stand looking over my father's shoulder, trying to tell him what to do, and his work on our hair was never satisfactory. So sometimes we would go around for a while with half a haircut because he would simply get frustrated and stop. "Okay, you do it! I'm done!" he'd say handing her the scissors.

Now that I am older and have a choice, I pay to have my hair cut. I loved one barber I had as an adult. This fellow was funny and I enjoyed talking to him, yet sometimes he would forget what he was doing. His scissors would begin to work on my ears. I couldn't stay with him. It didn't matter how much I loved him, because he was pruning more than barbering. Pruning is more than shaping.

Fred Craddock writes: Jesus' message is clear — *My Father is the vine dresser.* "The vine dresser comes into the vineyard with a knife and every plant is severely cut. Some are cut away because they are fruitless." Some are pruned ... in order to be more fruitful. "But how are we to know the difference?" Craddock asks. These experiences are painful. It is often the case that pruning, severing a debilitating branch, causing the loss of a burdensome thing or meaningless pursuit, is understood as being estranged from God — leaving believers angry, confused and hurt. Perhaps even the early church, facing difficulties as it was, needed to be taught that they could be facing *pruning,* for greater fruitfulness, and *suffering,* to be more fully grounded in Christ.[1] Churches that move through hardships often find increased commitment to mission, find power and vision because they have been pruned, because they have suffered, because they have become more fully grounded in Christ.

Or think of Jesus' story: A lawyer stood up and questioned him. "Teacher, what shall we do to inherit eternal life?" Jesus said to him, "What is written in the law, how do you read?" He answered, "You shall love the Lord your God with all your heart, with all your soul, with all your strength, and with all your mind. And your neighbor as yourself." And Jesus said to him, "You have answered right. Do this and you will live." But desiring to justify himself, he said to Jesus, "Who is my neighbor?" And Jesus told the story — the very familiar one. A man was going down the road from Jerusalem to Jericho and he fell among robbers and he was stripped and beaten. And they left him for dead. Now by chance a priest was going down that road ... you know the story. And then came a Levite down that road and looked upon the man ... you know that story. But then a Samaritan came down that road and he looked upon that man and he took pity on him (Luke 10: 25-37).

Oh, people of God, is it not true that sometimes God prunes away things which confuse us, which cause our lives to be diminished and the Church to be diminished? Is it not true that God takes our suffering and grounds us in Jesus to help us see with the eyes that Jesus saw? Lest we walk down the road and leave the one who has been beaten and broken in the ditch?

Where is our home? Do we think our home is at 346 Pattie Drive or some such address? Because of our grounding in Christ, is our field of vision bigger? In the words of the lyricist, "O Lord my God, when I in awesome wonder consider all the worlds thy hands have made. I see the stars, I hear the rolling thunder, thy power throughout the universe displayed. Then sings my soul, my Savior God to thee, How great thou art!"[2]

Where is your home? Is your home with him? Is your home in him? Is there pruning? — Yes. Is there suffering? — Yes. Is there glory and power throughout the universe displayed — Yes! Does our suffering ground us more fully in Christ? — Yes. Does our suffering connect us even more intimately with God? — Yes.

Where is your home? Where is your heart's true home? Abide in me and I with thee. I live with Jesus and so do you, and he lives with us. He prunes us and shapes us and frees us even in suffering to be fruitful. Thanks be to God who abides with us.

---

1. Fred B. Craddock, John H. Hayes, Carl R. Holladya, Gene M. Tucker, *Preaching The New Common Lectionary*, Year B: Lent, Holy Week, Easter (Nashville: Abingdon Press, 1984), pp. 204-205.

2. "How Great Thou Art," words and music by Stuart K. Hine, Burbank, CA: Manna Music, 1953, no. 77, *The United Methodist Hymnal.*

Books In This Cycle A Series

GOSPEL SET
And Then Came The Angel
Sermons for Advent/Christmas/Epiphany
William B. Kincaid, III

The Lord Is Risen! He Is Risen Indeed! He Really Is!
Sermons For Lent/Easter
Richard L. Sheffield

No Post-Easter Slump
Sermons For Sundays After Pentecost (First Third)
Wayne H. Keller

We Walk By Faith
Sermons For Sundays After Pentecost (Middle Third)
Richard Gribble

Where Gratitude Abounds
Sermons For Sundays After Pentecost (Last Third)
Joseph M. Freeman

FIRST LESSON SET
Between Gloom And Glory
Sermons For Advent/Christmas/Epiphany
R. Glen Miles

Cross, Resurrection, And Ascension
Sermons For Lent/Easter
Richard Gribble

Is Anything Too Wonderful For The Lord?
Sermons For Sundays After Pentecost (First Third)
Leonard W. Mann

The Divine Salvage
Sermons For Sundays After Pentecost (Middle Third)
R. Curtis and Tempe Fussell

When God Says, "Let Me Alone"
Sermons For Sundays After Pentecost (Last Third)
William A. Jones

SECOND LESSON SET
Moving At The Speed Of Light
Sermons For Advent/Christmas/Epiphany
Frank Luchsinger

Love Is Your Disguise
Sermons For Lent/Easter
Frank Luchsinger